ANSWER:
MEN ASK
AND THE ONES WOMEN WISH THEY WOULD

Every man has had moments of uncertainty
about how to touch a woman and when, about
what to say and when to say it, about timing,
positions, feelings, fantasies, and techniques.
Whit Barry talked to scores of women to find out
how they respond to everything from steamy
come-ons to tender words, from spontaneous
quickies to magical marathons of extended
sensual pleasure.

Beginning with that first spark between a man
and a woman through keeping sex exciting in a
long-term relationship, this exciting guide covers
all aspects of the lovemaking experience, including
complete information on orgasm and the G-spot,
and on how to develop the imaginative, sexually
stimulating delights of massage, deep kissing,
and touching her erogenous zones to reach the
ultimate erotic plateau that transforms "having
sex" into truly making love.

MAKING LOVE:
A MAN'S GUIDE

Ø SIGNET (0451)

FOR LOVERS ONLY

☐ **LOVE AND ADDICTION by Stanton Peele with Archie Brodsky.** This provocative book focuses on interpersonal relationships to explore what addiction really is—psychologically, socially, and culturally. "A rare book.—*Psychology Today* (141946—$4.50)

☐ **MAKING LOVE: A MAN'S GUIDE by Whit Barry.** What a woman really wants...and what makes it even better. The total guide for men to every stage of the lovemaking experience—and to a richer, more satisfying sexual life: Including new rules to turn the most intimate moments into the most arousing for her. Plus many more tips that every man should know to please a woman. (146840—$3.50)

☐ **MAKING LOVE: A WOMAN'S GUIDE by Judith Davis.** What does a man *really* want, anyway? You'll find all the answers in this one book that tells you how to turn your man on, including 20 sure-fire turn-ons to seduce him so he stays seduced; scores of gloriously imaginative ideas in the art of making love memorable; the well-known secret that kindles the steamiest sensual thrills; plus much, much more. (137329—$3.50)

☐ **HOW TO LIVE WITH A MAN: Everything a Woman Needs to Know by Caroline Latham.** Loving a man is not the same as living with one, and this warm, supportive no-nonsense guide shows you how to avoid the mistakes and solve the problems that can devastate your relationship, and how to deepen your joys and fulfillment. (131762—$2.95)

Prices slightly higher in Canada

Buy them at your local bookstore or use this convenient coupon for ordering.

NEW AMERICAN LIBRARY,
P.O. Box 999, Bergenfield, New Jersey 07621

Please send me the books I have checked above. I am enclosing $_____ (please add $1.00 to this order to cover postage and handling). Send check or money order—no cash or C.O.D.'s. Prices and numbers are subject to change without notice.

Name_____

Address_____

City_____State_____Zip Code_____

Allow 4-6 weeks for delivery.
This offer is subject to withdrawal without notice.

MAKING LOVE:
A Man's Guide

by
Whit Barry

②
A SIGNET BOOK
NEW AMERICAN LIBRARY

NAL BOOKS ARE AVAILABLE AT QUANTITY DISCOUNTS
WHEN USED TO PROMOTE PRODUCTS OR SERVICES.
FOR INFORMATION PLEASE WRITE TO PREMIUM MARKETING DIVISION,
NEW AMERICAN LIBRARY, 1633 BROADWAY,
NEW YORK, NEW YORK 10019.

Copyright © 1984 by Whit Barry

All rights reserved

Ⓞ

SIGNET TRADEMARK REG. U.S. PAT. OFF. AND FOREIGN COUNTRIES
REGISTERED TRADEMARK—MARCA REGISTRADA
HECHO EN CHICAGO, U.S.A.

SIGNET, SIGNET CLASSIC, MENTOR, PLUME, MERIDIAN AND NAL BOOKS
are published by New American Library,
1633 Broadway, New York, New York 10019

First Printing, June, 1984

4   5   6   7   8   9

PRINTED IN THE UNITED STATES OF AMERICA

Contents

CHAPTER ONE

What Can A Man Give A Woman?

The late-afternoon California sun casts long, golden rectangles on the oriental carpet in Susan's waiting room. Susan is a lawyer, specializing in domestic relations, and I am here to see her on a matter of some urgency.

When I was growing up in the Midwest, I knew Susan as my friend Al's older sister. She was serious, bespectacled, chubby, and friendly—popular in that "everybody's buddy" kind of way. She knew me as the smart-mouthed kid who was always shooting baskets with her brother in their driveway. I liked her because she was fun to tease and because she always spoke to me when we saw each other at school. She didn't really have to say anything, because she was a big wheel, and I was two classes behind her.

Years pass. I am in California, collecting information for a book on making love to women. For such a universal activity, it is turning out to be surprisingly susceptible to shifting cultural trends. Like everybody else, I realized that the traditional male-female roles had been superseded in the last decade by a newer, less rigid set of expectations. Everyone knows that today's women buy and sell companies, run governments, install pipelines, and race in the Indy 500. And everyone knows that women today can pay their own way, open their own doors, and fall behind in their own alimony payments. The world really has shifted in its thinking. Just watch a waiter carefully position the check—or the wine list—in that neutral territory between the man and the woman. He—or she—is no fool.

On the subject of making love, however, all is not so clear-cut. Somewhere between paying the check and slipping between the sheets, confusion has set in. As many men have discovered, just because a woman is a corporate powerhouse by day doesn't mean she wants to be treated like one at night. On the other hand, she isn't some sweet innocent young thing, either. Women are people, not things, sweet or otherwise.

Few men can really work up much energy to complain about the progress women have made. Most men I know, myself included, would admit their lives have become richer and more varied now that women are actively involved side by side with men in so many arenas where they were once denied access.

But—and it's a big "but"—men are at a loss to understand how they are supposed to handle these new male-female roles on a more personal level. What do women want from men? When it comes to making love, which of the old verities remain, and which no longer apply?

In certain circles, there is even some question of whether women need men at all. "A woman without a man is like a fish without a bicycle," Gloria Steinem says—to the cheers of her sisters, and the weak laughter of all the men who consider themselves liberated but who wonder just where liberation leaves them.

Obviously, women are no longer dependent on men for protection, or status, or a meal ticket. Does this leave only the grimly practical sexual urges that guarantee the continuation of the species? Is there no other need that draws men and women together? Nothing left that a man can give a woman?

Rules governing relations between the sexes suggest very few answers to these questions. As my friend Al exclaimed in great frustration over the long-distance lines late one evening, "Whenever I get involved with a woman, I feel like I'm playing a surreal game of chess. The players *look* the way they always have, but the rules change every two moves. Sometimes I think I'm dealing with the New Assertive Woman, and ten minutes later I get the definite impression I'm supposed to sweep sweet little her into my big strong arms."

Susan, he told me, had moved to San Francisco and become some kind of lawyer. "Why don't you give her a call and see what she's got to say?" he suggested. "I think domestic relationships are her specialty."

So I do, and now I am sitting in her waiting room.

It is part of a first-floor suite in a restored Pacific Heights Victorian house. The decor bespeaks success—that oriental carpet, oil paintings, tastefully selected antiques but as soon as she emerges from her office, it is Susan who captures my attention. Slim and fit, wearing an elegant white suit that sets off her California tan, she is not the chubby high-school yearbook editor I used to tease. It suddenly occurs to me that while Susan may be an expert on domestic relationships, she may also have some personal insights into the question at hand.

The silk underwear syndrome

"I've got news for you and Al," Susan said after I'd spoken my piece. "Women are just as confused as men are these days."

"But it's women who want new rules," I protested. "They're the ones who fight the double standard, who don't want to define themselves through relationships anymore, who—"

"Look," she interrupted. "Let's back up a little. There's tremendous pressure on both sexes today. We all pretend we've let go of those old Rock Hudson–Doris Day values, but few people really have. What's happened instead is that we've just added some new demands. Men try to be sensitive, open, and virtuosos of endless foreplay—while still believing, deep down, they must also be strong, in charge, and all those other masculine traits."

"Just like when we were in high school."

"Right. And the challenge women face is to charge forth, develop their assertiveness, make independent lives for themselves, and at the same time try to figure out just where their femininity really lies. Take a young professional woman today who—"

"Like yourself?"

She frowned at me, hands on hips, just like she used to do when Al and I had gone too far with our teasing, and then grinned broadly. "Okay, sure, like myself. You know how the more tailored a woman's clothes become, the sexier and more frivolous the underwear she buys?"

"Right," I agreed, hoping to sound offhand. "I have noticed that a lot, yes."

She laughed. "I'll bet you have. Anyway, I call it the silk underwear syndrome. What I mean is, I have a private practice, I argue cases in court, I do some teaching. I'm a professional, and I like to act like one. When it comes to my own relationships, though, I have a lot of trouble shifting gears."

"Shifting gears to what?" I asked.

"To ... I'm not sure I can say, exactly. Well, for instance, what if you and I were to have a relationship?"

"You and me?" I gulped, suddenly feeling like a high-school sophomore.

"Why not?" She laughed again. "You're the one who wanted to make this personal. Anyway, here you are, seeking my advice as an expert. Maybe I find you attractive—you're not bad, actually—and I ask you out to dinner. My treat. Any problems with that?"

"Uh, no."

"Me neither. So we have dinner. Maybe I even select the wine. Things work out and we go to my place, let's say. So far, the perfect 'new age' scenario, right? I'm even a little bit older than you. So there we are in bed, and I've got some ideas about what I'd like to do and I'm not shy about expressing them. So I do. And you like it. But . . ."

"But what? Don't stop now. It's just getting interesting."

She frowned, twisting a lock of auburn hair around her finger. "Well, it's just that at some point that wouldn't be enough. I'd want you to . . . 'take over' are the words that come to my mind."

"I think I could manage that."

"Yes, okay, but I'm not sure 'taking over' is exactly what I mean. This is the shifting gears part: even though I don't consider myself a passive female, for me to feel desirable, sexy, feminine, whatever, I need to feel . . . pursued. Pursued, and won over."

"The old caveman routine."

"Well, yes, in a way. In most of my life, I have no use for that stuff, and I really wouldn't want a relationship in which the man was dominant and I was submissive. But when it comes to making love, I want . . . something like that, at least some of the time. That's the problem. How do you shift back and forth, especially over a period of time, assuming our relationship goes anywhere?"

"With a special kind of man?" I suggested, wondering how I would measure up.

"I guess so," she replied, almost wistfully. "Special enough to make a woman feel like a woman and at the same time treat her like a person."

"That's quite a challenge you've set up."

"And I'll tell you something else, you and Al," she said. "I'm not the only woman who feels this way. There are a lot of us out there. Talk to a few women. You'll find out."

What do women want from a man?

"To make her feel like a woman, and to treat her like a person."

Susan was right. The more women I talked to, the more I found who felt the same way she did. While they weren't after caveman sex any more than Susan was, they wanted an experience that, as one woman described it, "brings a man and woman together by celebrating our differences as well as our similarities."

I asked them what, exactly, that meant. What were the approaches, techniques, physical attributes, and body types that turned women on? In other words, just what was it they wanted from a man?

Their answers (which I duly noted for inclusion in the book) covered the variety of men in the world: from the sensitive poet to the take-charge salesman, subtle or obvious, short or tall, intellectual or instinctive, boyish or sophisticated. But although each woman had her individual preference about the type of man she liked, type was not the bottom line. When I had taken a close look at everything they had told me, it turned out that what women wanted from men boiled down to three qualities, which, in combination, they could get from no other source. Men who were able to satisfy these three needs almost invariably earned high marks as exciting and sensitive lovers.

Validation

For most women, the ultimate measure of their appeal as women lies in the response of a man. Few women—no matter how successful and powerful—really want to be treated like one of the boys, at least not all the time. They want to be treated as women, unless they are uncomfortable with their sexuality in the first place.

This doesn't mean they want to be patronized, or fawned over, or forced into dealing with a constant barrage of sexual innuendos. It does mean they want to be appreciated as women. Sometimes it's just a matter of awareness. "I work with guys all day long," said a busy interior designer, "and I can tell when a man tunes in to me as a woman. There's nothing steamy, just a kind of unspoken appreciation. It makes me feel good. I find myself thinking, Kiddo, you've still got what it takes."

How does a man make a woman feel like a woman? From the wolf whistle to the cape laid across a mud puddle, men have devised endless stratagems to get their message across. It all comes down to how you respond—attentiveness, appreciation, gallantry—anything you do to let a woman know *you* know she is a woman and you like it. It's up to you to find the response that best fits your feelings, the woman, and the situation.

I found out, however, that hiding your feelings behind a macho facade won't get you very far these days. "I meet men all the time who come on like gangbusters," a woman told me. "I can tell they like me and would like to get acquainted, but they're afraid to expose themselves, and so they get sexual right away. I feel like telling them to back up and start over."

Women like men who can take a risk and expose their feelings. Everyone responds to openness far more readily than to any "line"—or to a specific lovemaking technique, for that matter. The men I talked to who were most successful with women were able to communicate their interest and desire in ways that were compelling without being offensive or overwhelmingly macho. Honesty is central to them all. Said one young building contractor, "I don't fake things. If I find a woman attractive, I just let that come out naturally. Any sexual undercurrents seem to take care of themselves, because I'm a man and she's a woman."

Caring

Everyone needs caring. That sounds obvious, yet many people—men, especially—are embarrassed to express the part of themselves that considers another person's needs, and responds thoughtfully. Also, in recent years, the gallantry and courtliness with which men were taught to treat women have fallen under a shadow. Some men have learned to withhold such gestures for fear they will be interpreted by the woman as patronizing—"the little lady is too tongue-tied to give her order directly to the waiter"—or manipulative— "candy's dandy, but liquor's quicker."

And gallantry certainly can be both condescending and a cover-up for hidden motives. When, during National Secretary's Week, a group of secretaries put up "RAISES, NOT ROSES!" posters, they were serving notice that they would not be bought off by once-a-year cheap displays of appreciation.

But no woman told me she objected to a man with good manners, or one who took the trouble to find out what pleased her or went out of his way to consider her needs. When offered with no strings attached, this kind of treatment not only makes women feel cared for, it makes them feel special.

Nowhere is such treatment more appreciated than in the act of making love. A man who makes the effort to learn how to please a woman in bed is showing her he cares about her pleasure as well as his. This is not the same as acquiring sexual expertise in order to impress or dominate women or to prove your masculinity. The difference is a matter of your focus. Do you concentrate on pleasing her or demonstrating your sexual prowess? If it's the latter, a woman will sense it immediately and draw back. If it's the former, she will respond with caring of her own.

Passion

No amount of information on making love to a woman can instill passion. That must come from you. But you can learn how to express it, how to create moments that invite it, and how to help your partner rise to the intensity of your feelings with passion of her own.

Passion separates having sex from making love. When you make love with a woman for the first time, the experience is both an ending and a beginning. It is the culmination of shared sexual energy that has been building for hours, days, or even years, bringing with it the slowly growing realization that something wonderful is going to happen between the two of you.

And when it finally does, making love is no longer an ending but a beginning—a shift, subtle or profound, into a new kind of intimacy in which shared physical pleasures heighten and intensify every emotion. The slopes and curves of your lover's body, the brush of warm breath in the hollow of your neck, a tongue tracing slowly down to your navel, and then beyond—every sensation becomes charged with feeling. In these moments time is forgotten, and the normal boundaries between two separate identities have no meaning.

During these moments we feel most alive. They are the moments we yearn for, the moments we hope we can build on to develop or deepen our love. They are moments worth pursuing.

CHAPTER TWO

Sex and Looks

Most men assume that, these days, there must be a feminine equivalent to the "tits and ass" conversations that they hold with each other. In talking to women, I didn't find this to be true. Exactly.

Women certainly appreciate masculine beauty, and most are not shy when it comes to talking about it. Many women buy "beefcake" calendars and books filled with photos of handsome men. Women don't, however, make the same kind of leap between physical appeal and sexual turn-on that men do, at least not in a vacuum. "I love to lie on the beach and look at all the men in their skimpy bathing suits," one woman told me, "but it's sort of like appreciating the lines of a Greek statue. For me to think of a man's looks in sexual terms, there's got to be some kind of vibe or personal connection between us."

Time and again, when I asked women what they found sexually attractive in a man, they would end up talking about abstract qualities like self-confidence, personality, attitude. Like most men, I had trouble accepting these statements at face value. Back in college, describing a potential blind date as having a "great personality" meant that she wasn't long on looks. I assumed that if I probed deeply enough, I would eventually arrive at what *really* turned women on. Was it muscles? Sexual performance? Awesome genitals? Movie-star looks? It had to be *something*. Surely the posters of Jim Palmer standing around in his underwear didn't find their way to the refrigerator doors of all those women on the basis of his personality.

Well, no, my informants admitted, although many of them claimed that they could tell from the expression on his face that he was a nice person. "You know," one forthright young woman said, "he looks like what my mother would call a catch. He's cute, he's sexy, he's got great eyes, but it's the overall impression of sincerity I like. I know it's only a picture, but he manages to make me feel he cares about me. That's what comes across and what counts."

Many women are reluctant to express their opinions on this subject around men. "If I'm in the presence of men," a young woman told me, "and I say something like 'I find men's hands attractive,' I imagine all the men secretly looking at their hands and thinking they're not attractive enough. Maybe I'm afraid they will stay away from me because I won't like them."

The message these women were giving me was clear: we will tell you what we find physically attractive in men, but only if you understand that our total response to men is by no means limited to—or even dictated by—how they look or how they perform in bed. "Really," one women told me in exasperation, "why is this so hard for you men to get through your heads? Don't you realize that many women distrust men who are too good-looking? I should think men would be relieved to know they don't have to look like Tom Selleck to turn women on."

Buns

Message received, I pressed forward in my quest. After all, there are a lot of men spending a lot of time developing and maintaining their bodies, and not just to ensure cardiovascular fitness, either. As a matter of fact, I was one of them. Were all those hours spent locked in the embrace of Nautilus machines wasted?

No. Women *do* know a sexy male body when they see one. And what seems to top the list of sexy physical attributes are bottoms. "Buns," a fortyish woman told me, cupping her hands in front of her. "There's nothing like cute buns. Nice and tight, even if they're a little more than a handful. That does it for me, especially when his pants are snug and well cut. Droopy drawers on even the best body are bad news."

Flat stomachs

Right up there with buns are flat stomachs. In fact if there are leg men and breast men, there may also be bun women and stomach women. Polls on what women find attractive about men's bodies consistently give these two features top ratings. "It's that neat, firm look I go for," a young nurse said, "with nothing hanging over the belt."

Men envy other men's muscles. For many women, however, a too heavily muscled body has little appeal. What does appeal to them is overall body tone and fitness. Women like men who take care of their bodies, but they are acutely aware of the fine line between a healthy desire to look good and rampant narcissism. As one woman put it, "I like men who take care of their bodies, but not if that's all they think about."

Part of what women find appealing about a man with a healthy body is the self-confidence and awareness of the physical that often goes with it. "I like a man who's comfortable with himself," a California graphic artist said. "If he's in good shape, he moves well—not swaggering, but as if he knew what his body was for. So long as it's not overbearing, I respond to a certain physicality in a man. It gets me thinking about what he might be like in bed. With me, of course."

Fitness and grooming

If you want women to respond to your looks, your first step is to take care of them. Fortunately, you needn't have been a college all-star to get in shape right now. Millions of men who never spent any more time in a locker room than they had to are discovering the joys of physical fitness. Exercise makes you look better and feel better. You can tighten up your stomach, work on a sagging rear end, and develop muscle tone. In the process you will learn what it feels like to take charge of your body. From this comes the self-confidence that women find far more sexually appealing in the long run than bulging biceps and rippling pectorals.

A well-toned body also performs better in bed. Men who get regular exercise say it makes their love-making longer, more exciting, and more intense. "I can feel more," one born-again athlete said. "My body turns into one big erogenous zone. Wow!"

Pay some attention to your grooming as well. When it comes to making yourself attractive to women, neatness counts. While the unshaven ruffian may have a certain appeal in feminine fantasies, up close women want their men well groomed. Clean hair is a must. "When I meet a man," one woman said, "I always wonder what it would feel like to run my fingers through his hair. But not if it looks dirty or greasy."

Don't forget your hands and nails, either. Hands are among the first things many women notice about a man. "There's something about a man's hands that tells me a lot about him," a children's book editor claims. "You can see if he's strong, or sensitive, and if he takes good care of himself."

The bottom line on your grooming may be that women take it personally. If you want to show a woman you care about her, take the time to look good. This doesn't mean you have to sink a fortune in clothes, or spend hours in front of your mirror. Just make sure you're clean, shaved, pulled together. If you show up looking as if you couldn't be bothered, that is exactly how she will take it. "Too much is too much," one woman said. "I'm turned off if he dresses up just so I can be an audience for him. What I like is the feeling I'm important enough for him to make a little extra effort to look special."

Eyes

Eyes have been called the windows on the soul. Elizabethan poets thought they emanated rays of love. All the women I talked to had a lot to say about men's eyes. "Intelligent," "sexy," "calm," "sparkling," "responsive," "kind"—these were just a few of the terms they used to describe the kind of eyes they responded to. What became apparent, however, was that your eyes assume importance to a woman to the degree they are focused on her. They are a link, in a sense, between her and your feelings.

A portrait artist told me that despite what people think, expression resides more in the mouth than in the eyes. "You can tell more from the slightest change in a man's mouth than anything about his eyes," she believes. "But when a man turns his gaze to me and looks at me—and I mean really looks—that's real contact. If it's the right man, I just melt."

So don't worry about the color of your eyes or how deep set they are. Consider rather what you can do with them and what they reveal about you. Charismatic people can make whoever they are talking to think they are better, somehow, than they had thought they were. Part of their secret is the ability to focus entirely on the person they are with. By the way you look into a woman's eyes—the steadiness of your gaze, your concentration on her to the exclusion of everything else—you are letting her know that at that moment she is the most important person in your life.

"I met my congressman at a fund raiser," a young graduate student said, "and I had an immediate sexual response to him. I realized later it was because for the brief moment we spoke, he gave me his full attention. I felt like the most beautiful and attractive woman in the room. His eyes never left mine. Having someone pay that kind of concentrated attention to you is devastating."

Confidence

The story goes that soon after Jacqueline Kennedy married Aristotle Onassis, one woman asked another, "But how could she? He's so much *shorter* than she is!" "Ah yes," replied her friend, "but not when he's standing on his money."

Money, and the power that flows from it, are potent aphrodisiacs for many women—and for many men as well. But if you ask women to explain this phenomenon, they will tell you that, as a purely sexual turn-on, it's not the money or even the power but the aura of self-assurance that often radiates from rich and powerful men. They will be quick to add that a man doesn't have to be a millionaire or a corporation president to send out such signals. "Deliver me from the wimps of the world," wailed a young Houston researcher. "Give me a man who knows how!"

Knows how to make love? Well yes, ultimately, but that's not what this woman meant. What she was looking for was a man who conveyed a sense of competence. "I know that some women respond to the little boy in a man," she said, "but I don't. I don't care if a man is rich or poor, just as long as he knows what he wants and is able to go after it without apologizing or agonizing. That's a very sexy quality for me. He's got to know who he is. It suggests he'll know how to take care of himself and I won't have to worry about damaging his fragile ego, in bed or out."

This quality has a lot to do with the attraction that intelligent men have for women. "Once you get out of high school, brains can be surprisingly sexy," a former cheerleader told me. "There's something about an intelligent man that makes me want to find out more about him. Maybe it's because they often are very curious about the world around them and yet at the same time they seem so self-contained. They're a kind of challenge."

Sensitivity

Modern men have gotten the message loud and clear that macho is out and sensitivity is in. They are discovering that being able to cry at the right moment gets them farther with women than any amount of John Wayne swaggering ever could.

Judging from the women I talked to, however, there is some evidence that in recent years sensitivity may have been oversold. Yes, a woman wants the man in her life to be considerate and sensitive to her needs—so much so that if this kind of sensitivity is missing in their relationship, the relationship probably won't last very long.

Women today, however, are no longer quite so grateful for this quality as they were ten to fifteen years ago. Today, many women simply assume it as a given in any man they're involved with.

"Men expect women to be aware of what they want and act accordingly, so why shouldn't women expect the same?" says one experienced midwestern real estate agent. "I resent it when a man advertises his sensitivity, as if that's all he has to do, 'be sensitive.' Actually, what a lot of men call sensitivity is just being passive. Where is it written that it's up to the woman to make a relationship happen?"

Real sensitivity, of course, is knowing what your partner wants before she does. One of the most truly sensitive men I know has this knack and is willing to act on it. Once he arranged an elaborate evening of dinner and the theater. When he picked up his girlfriend, she was exhausted and overwrought from a hard week on the job. He could see that what she really needed was some quiet time alone. So he drew a warm bath for her, and while she was in it he went out and bought a dozen roses. He left them on her coffee table with a loving note and a raincheck for a definite time the following week.

Do you measure up?

There's an old joke about a woman who, seeing her boyfriend naked for the first time, pointed to his less-than-enormous penis and sneered, "Who do you expect to satisfy with *that*?" To which he responded, with a smug little smile, "Me."

No woman would every say such a thing. Women just do not make that kind of association between sexual satisfaction and the size of their partners' genitals. It simply isn't how their minds and emotions work.

As a reflection of masculine fears, however, the joke is accurate enough. Men have read that women don't focus on the size of their penises. They have been told that when erect, all penises are more or less the same size. Since men do not usually get the chance to see other men's erect penises, they have no way of knowing whether this is true or not. It's a comforting thought, but if a man has any concerns in this department, he tends to wonder.

Even the best-adjusted men are conscious of how they measure up. They may not necessarily be obsessed with the matter, but as they stand in the locker room they take note of the guy coming out of the shower or changing his clothes at the next locker, and in some part of their minds, they think, "His cock is bigger—or smaller—than mine." And no matter what they have read about what women want, they all believe bigger is better. Bigger is more potent, more powerful, more masculine.

This is an area of vulnerability for all men. One of men's greatest fears is that today's liberated women have lost the traditional feminine reticence about discussing their partners' sexual equipment—and capabilities. Men imagine consciousness-raising groups in which women sit around and compare notes.

One man told me this fear had stopped him from asking out a woman in his office whom he found very attractive. "She's dynamite," he said, "beautiful, and witty, and never at a loss for something to say. That's what I like about her, but at the same time it makes me wonder if I'd be good enough, if you know what I mean. So I hold back."

Do women compare notes? Do they kiss and tell? Well, yes, certainly they do—but not in the way most men fear. When women talk about the men in each other's lives, it is usually in the total context of the relationship. Feelings, more than performance, equipment, or looks, form the basis for the conversations. Is the relationship emotionally satisfying? Does it seem to be going somewhere or is it temporary? What's going to happen next?

When women do emphasize the physical, it usually means the relationship does not play a big part in their lives. I know a woman who went through a postdivorce series of what she called her "butcher boy" affairs. Often they were younger than she—men in whom she had no lasting interest and who for a variety of reasons were clearly unsuitable. That, in fact, was their greatest charm. "I used to regale my friends with my 'hunk' stories," she says. "Sure, I talked about what we did in bed—and on the floor, and in the back of the van. My friends loved it. But if those guys had really been important, I wouldn't have talked like that. All that stuff would have been, well, irrelevant."

How to be sexy

What can you do about your fears of measuring up? One solution, of course, would be only to go after the type of woman who poses no threat to your fragile ego and whom you could completely dominate and control. The problem with this approach is that you might well be eliminating all the exciting, vital, attractive, and self-possessed women in the world.

A better approach would be to adopt the attitude of the man in the joke who aimed to satisfy himself— not his selfishness, certainly, but his self-confidence. To be the kind of man women find sexy *and* suitable does not require Kama Sutra lovemaking techniques, or a large bank balance, or even the prospect of one. You needn't be devastatingly handsome, or intellectually brilliant, or "a man among men."

But you can't just sit in a corner and tell yourself you're wonderful over and over and expect any results, either.

Start by getting comfortable with yourself—who you are, what you like, what you want. Instead of focusing on how you compare with other men, take stock of your own areas of strength and work on them. Granted, it may be easier said than done, but the payoff is tremendous in terms of your own inner well-being, and your relations with other people. When you are satisfied with yourself, you will project an aura that will make others want to be with you.

Develop your passions. Try some different activities on for size—not to meet women, but to find out what turns you on. Whether it be dirt-biking, politics, sailing, or organic gardening, the experience of going all out will spill over into your relations with women. When you elevate your emotional energy level, you will connect with other vital and exciting people in deeper, more satisfying ways. Women cannot help but respond to a man who gets totally and passionately involved with life. Such a man, they sense, could let himself get totally and passionately involved with them.

Get in shape. In addition to looking better, you'll feel better about yourself, and this self-confidence will be a powerful attractor. It's never too late. One man in his forties I talked to has become a Nautilus junkie, and it's paid off for him in more than just fitness. "I grew up assuming I was not the physical type. Working out has showed me I can take charge of how I look. My body *feels* different now—tauter, harder—and I like it better. I move differently, and I can definitely notice a difference when I'm making love. I use more of my body, and feel more, and let go more, I guess because I'm not so self-conscious."

Make friends with women. Today men and women have all sorts of opportunities for getting to know each other as people without first having to deal with the pressures of dating and sex. Don't write off a woman simply because you feel no immediate and compelling sexual attraction. If you like her, spend some time getting to know her. Who knows what can happen? If a relationship does develop, chances are it will be better and more long-lasting than one based primarily on sexual appeal.

Women like this approach. As one high-school teacher said, "I like men who like women as people, men who can get on my wavelength without any ulterior motives. There's no pressure, and things can just sort of develop at their own pace."

But without doubt the biggest step you will take toward being the kind of man women find sexy is to learn to focus your attention. *Be with* the one you're with. Even at the noisiest party, you can create a private oasis for just you and the woman you're talking to by focusing all your senses on her. Pay attention to what she's saying and feeling with her mouth, her eyes, her body. Let her know that for the moment, she's the only person in the room who exists for you. This means listening to her words, sensing her mood, and responding. As one woman put it, "If a man focuses all his attention on me—not in an intrusive way, but just by being totally responsive and accessible to me—I suddenly discover all sorts of things about him that are sexy and appealing. It happens every time."

CHAPTER THREE

Women's Sexual Hang-Ups

There is nothing more wonderful than making love to a woman who feels totally appreciated and cared for. Basking in the warmth of your tenderness, she can flow into the sexual experience with no fears or worries to hold her back.

"It's like floating in a warm pool," one woman said. "I feel totally open to him. Every word, every caress, every sensation goes right through me. During those moments, an orgasm can be almost beside the point. And of course, if it does happen, it's the best."

What stands in the way of this ideal is a whole host of concerns women bring to their lovemaking that keep them from relaxing completely. Few women, even the most articulate, feel comfortable talking about them with the men in their lives. Yet they all respond to lovers with the sensitivity to recognize them and act accordingly. "We women are taught to cater to men's sexual insecurities," an angry young advertising executive said. "Why can't they learn to do the same for us?"

As a man you can become more aware of how to deal with women's sexual fears by first thinking about your own—and then forgetting them. If you are like most men, you worry about performance: getting and keeping an erection, lasting long enough to satisfy your partner, orchestrating the experience. You may wonder if your sexual equipment is up to par, if your technique is polished enough, if you know the right buttons to push. Virtually all men can remember sexual encounters in which these worries reduced lovemaking to mere groin grinding, if they did not kill it off altogether.

The same is true for women. Women's fears are different, but their power to block off satisfying lovemaking is just as potent. By learning to help your partner set them aside, you can open her—and yourself—to moments of real sexual passion. You can become the lover many women fantasize about: the man who can overcome a woman's sexual hang-ups without having to be told what they are.

So what *are* a woman's major sexual hang-ups?

(1) "I worry about my attractiveness, especially my breasts."

For every woman embarking upon a sexual relationship, there comes the moment of literally naked truth: when my clothes are off, will he find me attractive? Am I too fat? Too thin? Does my stomach pooch out too much? Are my breasts firm enough? Big enough? Too big? "If I'm out with a man and I know we're going to end up in bed, I can get so uptight about my looks that the whole evening is ruined," one woman admitted.

No woman is too beautiful—or too militant a feminist—to be immune to the need to feel her lover is turned on by her body. Maria, a dynamite model, swivels heads whenever she's in public, yet she too worries about her appearance. "I defy you to find a woman who doesn't run numbers on herself about her looks," she claims. "I know I photograph well, but in the flesh I worry that maybe there isn't much flesh. Besides, you want to know a secret? No matter how many people tell you you're pretty, you need to hear it from the man you're with. If I'm in bed with a man who lets me know he finds me attractive, I forget about my bony knees or whatever and just blossom. It's a very very sexy feeling."

A man's response, then, is quite simple: tell her you find her attractive, and tell her again. Give her the specifics. Take the time to discover the secrets her body holds. Think of all her physical attributes that turn you on—soft skin, the juxtaposition of curves and hollows, special scents, the look and feel of her hair—and tell her. Better yet, show her. "I love the way your body feels when I run my hand down your back," you might say. "See? Like this."

Be sensitive to her needs. If she seems self-conscious about some part of her body, your compliments in that direction may only serve to emphasize her worry. Start by appreciating the parts of her you sense *she* feels good about, and go on from there.

Consider carefully what you say in her presence about other women's looks. Be warned that, quite naturally, she's going to take these comments as clues to your reactions to her. I know a man with the knack of saying just the right thing. "She does have nice legs, doesn't she?" he'll say to his partner, giving her a loving squeeze. "They remind me of yours."

For most women, breasts are the objects of greatest anxiety. It's often said that as a focus for sexual insecurities, breasts are to women what penises are to men—with the difference that many women think their breasts are too large. As one psychiatrist put it, "As far as women are concerned, breasts come in 'too' sizes: too small or too big."

It's no wonder. Women see men ogling large breasts or making jokes about "big knockers" and assume these attributes (often the product of the airbrush and/or the surgeon's skill) are necessary to being considered attractive. What they need to know is that such "did you see those tits" behavior is more a crude attempt by men to prove their manliness (to themselves and other men) than it is a comment on their actual preference. The fact is that just as breasts come in all shapes and sizes, so do men's—and each man's—preferences.

So how do you make her feel comfortable about

her breasts? First, if you think she's self-conscious in any way, don't make a big deal by trying to argue her out of her concern. Just show her. "I love it when a man fondles my breasts," a woman said, "when I feel the warmth of his hands on them. It's not the same if they seem to be something he's 'after.'"

Instead of focusing all your attention on her breasts, include them in your caresses of her entire body. Run your tongue around their swell. Capture her nipples in your mouth. Press your chest gently against hers and experience the simultaneous sensation of soft breast and hard, erect nipple. Show her you appreciate her breasts as part of *her*.

(2) "I worry that you don't really care about me."

There are some women who claim to relish an occasional one-night stand. "As long as I feel safe, it can be deliciously wicked and free, a ships-passing-in-the-night sort of thing," a salesperson for a computer firm reports. "As long as I make sure I don't feel *used*."

"Being used" stands as one of modern women's greatest sexual fears. At its root is a feeling of powerlessness. Emotionally more open than most men, women often find themselves with all their cards on the table, facing men who are playing theirs close to the chest.

Many women today go to great lengths to make sure this doesn't happen to them—sometimes to the point of shying away from serious relationships entirely. "No more of that 'take me, I'm yours' routine" is the general response. "Caring has got to be a two-way street."

Sonya is a ravishingly beautiful and talented dress designer who lived for years on a small farm fifty miles outside San Francisco and had no trouble sell-ing all her work to a few exclusive shops in the city. Recently she moved into a large, sun-washed flat in town, where she is more accessible to her customers and closer to the local fashion scene. However, she believes the real reason for her move has more to do with her changing attitudes toward men than anything else.

"When men think you're good-looking—and when they think other men think so too—all kinds of weird things happen," she says. "Number one, you get a lot of attention. Men hit on you all the time. Nice, you say? Not really, not after a while. They don't really know who you are. Most of the time they're not even interested, and the ones who might be are scared off.

"Number two, you become a kind of blank screen they project all their 'I'm going out with a beautiful woman' fantasies on. Number three, you get very, very leery. That's what happened to me. I literally had to leave town to get my head straight."

She says she owes her eventual reentry to Stan, a local contractor she met when her farmhouse needed some repairs. "We'd sit around and drink coffee during his work breaks and my work breaks, and just talk," she says. "He was so patient and sensitive and understanding of where I was. I'd never had a man demonstrate that kind of caring about me before without having an ulterior motive."

To show a woman you care about her, you need to open up. More than flowers and candy, women want partners who can let down their guard and acknowledge their feelings. "There's nothing that makes me feel closer to a man than his willingness to be human with me," one woman said. "I don't just mean crying on my shoulder or telling me all his problems, but being *real*. If he can do that with me, I know I'm important to him."

So be responsive. There are more ways than achieving an erection to show her the effect she's having on you. When you're in bed with a woman, let her know how you're feeling—not in the form of minute-by-minute bulletins but in whatever way seems appropriate to the mood. It may be a sigh, a look, a sudden grin. You'll both feel closer for it.

Be considerate. If she's tired or upset, don't press for sex. What she may need at that moment is holding and closeness, the connectedness of body warmth and unspoken thoughts running in the same direction.

A big part of being considerate is thinking about birth control. In this day and age, many men simply assume that the fear of pregnancy no longer exists among women. Not so. It's a fear not far from many women's minds. Modern birth-control methods are by no means danger-free, as research has amply demonstrated. Women resent being the ones who always have to take responsibility in this area, especially when it means putting their own health at risk. Raise the issue with her. Let her know you accept your responsibility, and decide together the steps you will take.

If this all sounds like good lovemaking goes hand in hand with some kind of personal response and caring, you're right. The closer the two of you are, the better the lovemaking. Love, openly expressed, is the best aphrodisiac of all.

(3) "I'm afraid I'm not up to the sexual demands you may make."

Do women want to be swept away?

Yes and no. Most women, especially those who are young and inexperienced, appreciate a knowing lover in whose arms all their awkwardness and uncertainties simply melt away.

There is a fine but critical line, however, between being masterful and being domineering. Fantasies aside, women fear being physically dominated, especially when they don't know what to expect. "A man's size and strength can be very exciting," a college student said, "but I don't like to feel I'm being forced into anything. Then I panic."

Said another woman, "Sometimes a man's sexual needs can be so *intense*. I had the experience of being with a man who seemed to turn into another person when he made love. He just lost control—he was so desperate and greedy—and I suddenly realized I had no idea of what he might do. Men should know that when a woman makes love, she feels at her most vulnerable, physically as well as emotionally."

Another aspect of this worry, common among many women who think of themselves in other areas of their lives as fairly sophisticated, stems from simple ignorance. Despite the sexual revolution, more women than you might imagine—and more men too—have no real experience with many of the lovemaking techniques they have read so much about. Yet the types of relationships they would like to have demand a certain level of sexual sophistication.

Or so they fear. Meg, blossoming into a career as a spokesperson for a high-powered lobbying organization, calls the dilemma "experience lag." "Most of my life I was achievement-oriented," she says. "I missed out on a lot of the boy-girl stuff that teenagers get into, and I just haven't had a lot of experience with very many men. Now I have a job where I meet a lot of men, and they probably think I know more than I really do. There are times when I hesitate to get involved because I'm afraid my ignorance will show. I wonder if I know as much as I should about what men want from a sexual relationship, and what I should do."

Women still feel, whether it's true or not, that men are more experienced sexually than they are. As a man, you may have an experience lag of your own. Whether you do or not, however, you should be aware of the phenomenon as women experience it. Take every opportunity to let her know you will not push her into doing something she doesn't feel ready for.

Oral and anal sex are the big bugaboos for a lot of

women. Thanks to *Deep Throat* and countless magazine articles, their curiosity may have been aroused. They may be willing to experiment, but they do not want to be rushed.

The secret is to go slowly. Show her, gently, the pleasures of cunnilingus for both the giver and the receiver. Make sure she realizes that the future of the relationship does not depend on her willingness to perform fellatio. If you allow time for her to minister to your needs, the matter may evolve naturally. In other words, don't push her head down. Try simply lying back and seeing what develops. If she is allowed to be in charge, she can do as much as she's comfortable with. The first few times you might want to stop her before you ejaculate.

One man reports success with a messy but, he claims, effective technique involving grape jam. "It was my girlfriend's idea, actually," he said. "She put some on the end of my erection, and licked it off before it ran down to the bottom. Then she took my penis in her mouth. I tried not to thrust at all, so she wouldn't be afraid of choking. It was great!"

(4) "I worry that I won't be in the mood."

Yesterday's sexual customs supported extended and romantic preliminaries. Women, perceived as delicate creatures, were to be won over, coddled, and "romanced" into "bestowing their favors," and it was up to the man to set the stage for this to happen.

The sexual revolution, by emphasizing the equality between men and women, has given these preliminaries a bad name. They seem to smack too much of manipulation. Liberated women, the new theory goes, "know what they want," and are demeaned by the slow buildup.

Wrong. The fact is, women—and men—may need it more than ever. "I've got a million things to think about at work," says Peggy, a successful assistant district attorney. "So does Bob. When we get together in the evening, we both need decompression time. I can't shift gears from business to sex on a moment's notice. Sometimes I really want to be with him, but I don't want the pressure of thinking I've got to feel sexy in forty-five minutes."

Being sensitive to the pressures she may be under is the first step in establishing the right tone. Without this sensitivity, stage setting will simply seem like an attempt to manipulate her into going to bed with you.

Use your imagination to come up with places to go and things to do that will help you both relax and get in the mood. Instead of a movie, why not a hot tub and massage in one of the many facilities for such activities that are springing up around the country? Or try out your mutual massage skills on each other. If you make it clear that sex is not the expected outcome, the experience can be nurturing for both of you.

Howard, an enterprising but far from affluent engineer, believes in fewer but more extended periods of time together. "I'd much rather spend a day or weekend away from home than exhaust my funds on a lot of dinner dates," he claims. "If we go away—bicycling, or looking at antiques or just sight-seeing, we both can relax and have more fun. We run around all day Saturday, have a leisurely dinner somewhere romantic, and go back to our hotel or inn. Then we're both in the mood for some fantastic lovemaking. Sometimes we spend all day Sunday in bed. That's quality time: no rush, no pressure, just time to enjoy each other."

(5) "Sometimes all I want is physical tenderness, not an orgasm."

One of the most misinterpreted cues women send out concerns their need for physical tenderness. "Gary has just two responses when I tell him I want to be held," Pam says. " 'No,' or 'sex.' Sometimes I think he's a penis walking around with a body attached."

Bernie Zilbergeld, sex therapist and author of *Male Sexuality*, believes this is a conditioned rather than an innate response. Push a man's physical tenderness button, Zilbergeld says, and he responds sexually. It's part of the macho training he's received from the culture. He's learned that doing anything less is a sign of impotence.

You can unlearn this behavior. Start by taking her at her word. Be affectionate. If it's closeness she asks for, give it to her. You can hold her, caress her hair, and provide the tenderness she may need from you without having to prove your manliness by becoming sexual. If you feel yourself getting aroused, don't assume you have to do anything. If you don't feel sexual, don't worry that there's something wrong with you. You may just be sensitive enough to appreciate her needs of the moment. And the next time, when both of you feel like making love, it will be better than ever.

CHAPTER FOUR

The First Spark

Sometimes it happens just as the song says, across a crowded room. At other times the setting is a laundromat, a busy street, your dentist's waiting room, the all-night grocery. Out of nowhere, when you were least expecting it, you catch sight of someone who ignites a sexual spark within you. What caught your attention? Was it a glance that lingered one moment too long to be casual? A gesture? A throaty laugh, spontaneous and uncensored? A fragrance that speaks to you of gardenias and tropical evenings?

Whatever the trigger, you find yourself awash in unsettling feelings that powerfully disturb your equilibrium. Almost simultaneously you experience an urge to move in, get closer, make contact—and a sudden fear that the object of your interest, that total stranger who has so quickly become so important to you, will rebuff your advances. You live for a moment with your indecision, relishing the anticipation but fearing to make any move that could spoil your fantasy.

As you sense the tension building within you—seconds? minutes? hours?—you look desperately for some sign from her that she returns your interest. Does she move closer? Glance again in your direction? Or will be up to you? You search your mind frantically for a suave approach she will find irresistible, but what comes out is a big awkward smile over which you feel little control and some stupidly transparent question: "Do you come here often?" "Is this when the bleach goes in?" "Can you tell me if these avocados are grown in Florida?"

No matter. Something in your manner—possibly the obvious sincerity that has made you so tongue-tied—catches her interest, long enough, at any rate, for her to respond. She looks at you, says something flip, or serious, or equally awkward—and with a rush of adrenaline you think you see an additional blush of color in her face and slightly dilated pupils. You have made contact.

That is one kind of first encounter.

Another kind—more common, perhaps, but equally as earth-shaking—happens between two people who have known each other for some time. Say you are working late with a colleague on a report. Something about the light on her hair falling across her face as she bends over a set of figures catches your eye. You find yourself staring at her, chin in your hand. With an unconsciously feminine movement you have seen hundreds of times before but which now seems staggeringly sexy, she tosses back her hair and starts to say something. The intensity of your gaze stops her, however, and in that brief but telling moment of silence, each of you knows—and knows the other knows—that a subtle but irreversible shift has taken place.

You have made contact.

New Age romanticism

In the past, these heady moments would signal the beginning of an intricate sexual minuet, in which each partner's moves were known and understood ahead of time. He would speak first, she would blush and turn away. He would send flowers and come calling, she would sit in the parlor and cast warm glances in his direction.

There was a time when this elaborate dance struck

us as restrictive, dishonest, and even unhealthy. Today we're not so sure. Today you sometimes can't tell the difference between a date and an appointment.

"Nobody can read the signals anymore," one studio musician said, echoing the thoughts of many other women—and men as well. "Who's supposed to make the first move? I mean, if you're a hip woman, it's not supposed to be a big deal, right? But it is. And the men ... they're so afraid of being called sexist and insensitive they lay back. Sometimes no one does anything. If that's being hip, you can have it."

Men face the same dilemma. "No one likes to be rejected," one guy said, "but at least the old rules of the game kept things short and sweet. You asked, she said yes or no, you decided if she was serious, and then you took it from there. Now, you're supposed to 'relate as people,' whatever that means. If you reach for the check, you're playing some macho game. I don't get it."

One of the cruelest paradoxes, according to Eileen, a therapist friend of mine, was spawned in the touchy-feely days of the human-potential movement. "I see a lot of clients who worry because they are so concerned about social-sexual etiquette," she claims. "They think if they were doing it right, they would somehow just be able to 'go with the flow' and 'relate to the other person, consciousness to consciousness,' without giving any thought to the practicalities of how it would happen. This is New Age romanticism. It sounds nice, but life just doesn't work that way. People need some rules and guidelines."

Setting the stage

The first step in creating significant first encounters for yourself is to become familiar and comfortable with the unspoken language you need in order to make contact with the opposite sex. Women seem to be more at home with this language than men are; some men, in fact, are not consciously aware of its existence at all. It is partly body language and partly a fragile back-and-forth rhythm of words, silences, gestures, glances, and touches. The big advantage of this language is that each person can either escalate or derail the "communication" at any point—without ever having to admit that a communication has taken place.

If this sounds to you like flirting, you're right—in a way. You can think of flirting as its most advanced form—a high-stakes game that we'll get to in a minute—but flirting has overtones of coyness and sexual game playing that are not always appropriate to many situations where men and women meet today.

The fact is that while men and women complain that it's hard to "meet people" today, we are meeting members of the opposite sex all the time—more, probably, than in the past. The difference is that these meetings occur in the course of business or other daily routine, where no one can really afford to muddy the waters by injecting a note of sexuality. To do so would raise a host of unpleasant issues, ranging from "inappropriate behavior" to sexual harassment. As one young man just starting out as a sales rep for management training courses said, "I meet loads of attractive ladies every day, but it's all in the line of work. I hesitate to make any moves because I don't want to screw up a sale—and also because I don't want to get accused of using romance or sex as a sales technique."

The situation is worse for women. Having struggled so hard for acceptance on their merits, women are reluctant to "slip back," as they sometimes see it, by allowing themselves to consider the men they meet during the course of their work as potential romantic partners. "I guess I go overboard sometimes to maintain a strictly business attitude," one buyer told me, "in order not to seem like I'm using feminine wiles to get ahead."

Without coming on as a water-cooler Romeo, you can learn to make contact with women in ways that set the stage for a more personal relationship—sooner or later, whenever it seems to be appropriate. Start by becoming aware of unspoken signals women may be sending in your direction. When she talks to you, does she frequently touch her hair? Does she seem to find opportunities to make brief physical contact? Does she hold your gaze a moment longer than she has to?

These are not necessarily come-ons, nor should you take them that way and move in for the kill. Think of them rather as indications that she is responding to you as a man, as well as a colleague or sales contact or whatever. Allow yourself to respond in kind, if that is your inclination. Don't be afraid to put some warmth in your voice. Show your enthusiasm when you see her. If you feel like smiling, smile. Let her know without getting heavy that you find her attractive as a woman.

This isn't flirting. But it can add a certain spice to your daily life without requiring you to declare yourself of make overtures that may not fit the time or place. At this stage you should not be physical or seductive. What you *should* be is appreciative, accessible, aware, and ready for whatever might happen next. "There's a guy in my office I've got my eye on," one woman told me. "The other guys either work like automatons or come on too strong. But Tom—I don't know, he just sort of seems to take me in as a total person. I like being around him. It doesn't feel sexy, exactly, but someday, when the time is right, I bet we get together."

Serious flirting

During what one writer has called the high holy days of the women's movement, flirting fell out of favor. Too indirect, too manipulative, said the feminists. Today, however, it's making a comeback. A new generation of men and women are discovering the joys of sexual badinage without worrying about whether they are straying from the party line. Flirting is sexy and safe—but not so safe as to be boring.

One of the best things about flirting is that you can enjoy it for itself or as a route to real sexual intimacy. For some people it's an end in itself. An attractive bank teller I spoke to makes a game of it. "I love to flirt with an attractive guy," she says. "I like being able to hold my own with him, to return his lines with lines of my own. I like the feeling of power that I get when I make him respond to me."

Flirting can feel good, like stretching your muscles before a workout. Here are some simple rules you can follow to get your flirting skills in good shape.

Keep it light. The whole point of flirting is that it's a game in which each player skates near the edge of getting serious with the option of veering back to safety at the last minute. You don't necessarily need a bag of Noel Coward witticisms. Sincerity definitely has its place, so long as it doesn't get out of hand. "What woman doesn't like thoughtful compliments, the kind that shows a man has really paid attention to her?" a Japanese nurse said to me. "A man I once met at a party told me my hands were made to hold a painted ivory fan. It sounds silly, I know, but almost every time I look at my hands I think of his remark."

Be careful of overt sexual innuendo. There's a difference between setting up a pleasant undercurrent of sexual tension and forcing the issue. You can achieve the former through your attentiveness, body language, and tone of voice. At this stage, most women find overtly sexual remarks offensive.

On the other hand, I talked to a few women who relished the give-and-take of racy dialog, which they say they often initiate just for the shock value. "I once walked up to a guy at a Christmas party and told him he looked like he'd be fun to get in trouble with," a red-haired art teacher reported. "It set him back a bit at first, but it sure cut through a lot of the preliminaries."

Do you understand body language?

Experts on male-female interactions say there is an observable sequence of physical behaviors, almost as ritualized as a mating dance, that men and women go through to signal their sexual interest in someone new. When the behavior of both parties is in sync, they proceed toward sexual intimacy. When one or the other partner fails to pick up on a cue, the result is often a frustrating and puzzling dead end.

These same experts claim that, by and large, women are more attuned to these nonverbal communicators than men are. "I've seen men mess up time and again," says one San Francisco behaviorist who does a lot of his research in some of the city's best-known singles bars. "A guy'll be talking to a woman who is making all the right body gestures to indicate her interest, and he just blows it. He'll turn away at the wrong time, or talk when he should be quiet, or fail to reach out to her when she signals she's ready, and then he doesn't know why nothing happened."

In his article "Flirtation—the signals of attraction—deciphered" (*Vogue*, February, 1982), Timothy Perper, Ph.D., has divided the act of flirting into four stages, each leading to greater intimacy than the one before. For a flirtation to be "successful," he says, both partners must move through each stage together.

The first is the approach, when a couple begins talking. Then comes "swivel," when they turn and focus their attention exclusively on each other. This is followed by the crucial stage of "synchronization," when their movements unconsciously begin to mirror each other's. If the woman reaches for an hors d'oeuvre, for example, and the man does the same, their synchronized movements have the unconscious effect of drawing them closer together. On the other hand, if the man takes a sip of wine instead, at an unconscious level he is sending out distancing rather than closeness signals, and will therefore unwittingly short-circuit the connection he may be trying to establish with her.

The last stage is touching. During this stage, no touch is accidental—a leg brushed while shifting weight, a hand touched when passing a napkin—they are all invitations to greater physical contact. If they are not reciprocated or acknowledged, the relationship is likely to stall and peter out.

Experts have identified several distinct body movements that indicate someone wants to move to the touching stage. A woman may put her hand on the table near the man's or wipe the condensation slowly, almost hypnotically, off her glass. She may absently run one hand down her arm or repeatedly smooth out her dress. One of the most common unconscious come-hither signals is touching the hair.

Train yourself to pay attention to such clues. All these messages are telling you she's interested and wants to proceed—not necessarily directly to bed but certainly to the next stage in developing a relationship with you.

I talked to one guy who had gotten the word from an ex-girlfriend and had learned to profit from it. "Doris and I had moved from being involved with each other to just being good friends," he said, "and one day she let her hair down and told me about the time we had first met—but from *her* point of view. It was at a party. The first I really remember her was when we had a long conversation, toward the end of the evening, but she said she had been aware of me from the moment she had seen me.

"Then, with a little help from her, I started to remember times during the evening when I had brushed against her at the buffet, or heard her laugh, or caught her eye.

"She said she was just 'sending out vibes.' It sure took me long enough to pick them up. Now I'm a little faster on the uptake. I'm more aware of the women around me. I always stop and tune in to see if there are any 'vibes.' A lot of the time there are."

Getting together

Leslie was lamenting the inadequacies of the English language. "Here I am, a highly paid consultant. I have an executive assistant and a secretary. Last year I bought my first piece of investment real estate. Why do I still have to go out on 'dates'? Isn't there some other word that doesn't sound so much like a sock hop?"

Not many people actually make direct use of the word anymore, as in "Would you like to go out on a date?" These days, it's "How about dinner Thursday?" or "Lou and I went out last night," or "Want to get together over the weekend and do something?"

Whatever you call it, though, your first planned social occasion with a woman can set the tone for the entire relationship. It's well worth taking some time to ask yourself a few basic questions up front, even before you decide on what you want to do and where you will go.

First of all, what kind of impression do you want to create about yourself? For example, while you may like the low-risk approach of just "playing it by ear," you should know that few women are going to be as impressed with your imagination and interest in them as they would be if you took the trouble to make some plans. "I like a man who has the gumption to set up an evening," a Boston secretary said. "Even if it's not something I would find interesting, I respect him for taking the chance. It's this 'Oh, I don't know, what do *you* want to do?' stuff that turns me off."

Of course it's best to come up with plans that she *will* enjoy, because they let her know you care enough about her to have paid attention to her likes and dislikes. If you know she likes animals, for example, you might put together a picnic lunch and go to the zoo. If she likes old furniture, take her to that little restaurant that boasts French country antiques.

Second, how much money should you spend? All other things being equal, a woman cannot help but respond to an elaborate night on the town—partly for the sheer glamour of it but mostly because of what it says about your feelings for her. Not having a big bankroll needn't stop you, however. In fact, a showy display can sometimes backfire by putting unwelcome pressure on her to "come across" later in the evening.

The secret is to find ways to show her you care enough to exert a little imagination and effort. A medical student friend of mine, with more creativity than cash, invited a woman to go driving in the country in his venerable Fiat convertible. A few days before their date, he sent her a note reminding her of their engagement. In the envelope was a simple white silk scarf—"to get you in the mood for our flight," the note said.

Another friend likes to do some advance planning before taking a woman to a restaurant. A few days before their date, he'll phone the restaurant, arrange the menu (he always asks if the chef has prepared some special off-the-menu dishes), and have some flowers sent to the table. "It makes the woman feel special," he says. "She doesn't have to worry about what to order, and it really doesn't cost very much more. In fact, the whole experience is much more pleasant and less expensive than if we went to a really fancy place."

Finally, ask yourself what you are trying to achieve in the first place? Aside from just an opportunity to trade facts about each other, a first date is the time to become more physically comfortable with each other—not sexually, necessarily, but physically. Instead of going to a movie, in other words, why not go dancing? An evening of dancing, if you enjoy it, is a marvelous way to get acquainted and get physical at the same time.

You can apply the same approach to a simple weekday lunch in the park near your office building. Instead of having sandwiches, stop by a gourmet deli and buy some bread and cheese, some pâté, and perhaps an interesting salad or two. Then, instead of simply sitting and munching, you can share your food, prepare tidbits for each other—and even feed each other tasty samples. It's an opportunity for easy, nonthreatening physical contact. "There's something about having someone feed you a bite of something that can be very sexy and sort of innocent at the same time," one woman told me. "I feel like a young bird, but also like I'm in that erotic eating scene from *Tom Jones*."

Lunching

I have a male friend who practically gives lectures on the subject of lunches as the perfect setting for a first date. In the first place, he says, a lunch is usually less expensive than dinner. Furthermore, in the middle of the day there are less "what's going to happen when we leave the restaurant" worries, enabling both people to relax and simply enjoy each other in the moment. Also, he claims something happens during a long lunch that doesn't happen at dinner. "Go to a restaurant at lunchtime," he says, "and if you stay beyond the usual hour or so, you will notice a shift. The crowd thins out, the people who stay sit back and relax, and the whole mood of the place changes. It gets more intimate, more personal, and if you're there with a woman, it just carries you both right along with it. If you can't take the time during the week, try a weekend lunch or brunch. And don't be surprised if you end up enjoying love in the afternoon."

CHAPTER FIVE

Making Her Feel Like Making Love

The old-fashioned movie hero always knew just exactly when and how to sweep the heroine off to bed. There were no missed cues, no anxious chatter, no awkward pauses. He could read her every hesitation, sigh, and flutter. He knew just when to kiss her passionately and when to hold her quietly against his manly chest. So total was his mastery of the situation that by the time the screen faded to black (remember, this is an old-fashioned movie), we in the audience knew that perfect, passionate lovemaking was assured.

Short of hiring your own stable of screenwriters, what can you do to guarantee the same results?

First of all, realize that you are embarking upon a two-stage process. Before you can physically arouse a woman, you must make her *want* to be aroused. This sounds self-evident, yet many, many women complain that men spend most of their energy on the arousal stage and not nearly enough on putting them in the mood.

Mental foreplay

This is not physical foreplay, which we'll get to later. What I'm referring to here is seduction or what we might call *mental* foreplay. According to many of the women I talked to, it has become something of a lost art in recent years—due, they claim, to a combination of more relaxed sexual standards and the influence of feminism. "I miss the romancing, the things my mother told me my father did when they were dating," said a young New York woman in her thirties. "Relationships are supposed to be direct and honest today. 'Cut and dried' is another way of looking at it."

Many a man has managed to talk a woman into bed, congratulating himself on having made another conquest. "See?" he says. "I knew she didn't really mean it when she said no." But in the back of his mind he wonders why the experience was not more rewarding. He goes over and over his performance, searching for the answer. Wasn't I gentle enough? Too gentle? Did I rush into intercourse too fast? Should I have suggested/avoided oral sex? Did I last long enough to satisfy her?

According to the women I talked to, these are the wrong questions. "Honestly," one young management trainee lamented, "sometimes it's easier just to go to bed with a guy, even if you don't particularly feel like it, than to go through the hassle of saying no."

Says my friend the psychotherapist, "It's harder these days for a so-called liberated woman to make the point of how important it is that she *feel* like making love. There's the notion that, like a man, she's supposed to be more or less ready all the time. And if she's not, the answer is to get out her vibrator, or have the man perform some amazing and lengthy feats of physical stimulation. The stuff that used to go on *before* people got into bed has somehow gotten a bad name—too indirect or corny or something."

For a woman to *feel* like making love, she needs to feel both excited by the possibility, and relaxed and unthreatened at the same time. This is where your sensitivity comes in. Perhaps the best advice at this point is to be attentive and ardent—certainly ardent— but to take it one step at a time. If, for example, you lean over and whisper something in her ear during dinner—"the way your eyes pick up the candlelight in here is really driving me crazy"—give her a chance to take in and savor your remark before you proceed further.

Anticipation is a powerful aphrodisiac, and it is the name of the game here. As you let her know the impact she is having on you, you are creating all sorts of possibilities in her mind about what might happen next. In the process of turning them over in her mind, she is, consciously or unconsciously, making the decision about what she *wants* to happen. Don't interrupt this process by moving too quickly. You will be denying her the pleasures of her imagination and perhaps pushing so hard she will begin to resist.

"When I know a man is interested in me in a sexual sense," a busy Chicago business consultant said, "I start to think about him in a new way. I enjoy the attention and the flattery—I suppose that's how I know—but part of me is sort of sitting back and wondering, What will it be like with him? What will happen? How will I feel? That's almost the most delicious part, in a way. I'm getting myself in the mood, I guess."

Notice her words. She is getting *herself* in the mood. That's the process that you want to set in motion, and then encourage and sustain, but never rush.

Is there any room for the romantic gesture, the flamboyant gift, the element of surprise? Certainly, if you feel you are aware of her and the state of your relationship. In some cases, a bold and creative move on your part can be very effective. One young woman returned to her office after lunch one day to discover an orchid plant on her desk, sent by the man she had met at a party the night before and had been raving about to her colleagues that morning.

"It made me so happy," she said. "I was thinking that I had been running on a little too much about him. But when I saw the orchid, I realized I had made as much of an impression on him as he had on me."

On the other hand, exactly the same gesture had

the opposite effect on a stock analyst in San Francisco. "The flowers were embarrassing," she said, "because they made everything so public, and I had to explain to everyone in the office. It felt like pressure more than anything else."

You can never go wrong with just showing your feelings, even silently. Sometimes silence at the right time can be more exhilarating and sexy than words or extravagant gifts. "The first time I went out with Hank," Edie said, "he seemed tongue-tied. I'd look up and find him just staring at me. Then he'd get embarrassed and laugh, and I'd break up, and we'd just sit there with these idiotic grins on our faces. We probably looked stupid, but I loved it. We both knew what we were so excited about."

Sustaining the mood

Seldom are beds available just exactly when and where you would like them. Knowing how to sustain the mood, in other words, is a major part of learning how to make love to a woman. The time between the opening act and the main event can be minutes, hours, days, or weeks. Nothing is more frustrating than having passions cool and the mood lost.

You don't have to keep the sexual fires white hot. The trick to keeping the feelings alive is to maintain contact. "One of the times I like best is being with a man I'm considering making love with later that night," a weaver who lives in Berkeley told me. "If we're in the car going to his place or my place, I like to be touching him—my leg against his, or holding hands. I like the physical contact with him, but I almost prefer it if we're not making out wildly at every traffic light. Sometimes I just like the time alone with my thoughts about what might happen—as long as I know he's there."

Let her know you're there, but don't overdo it. If you're in public, be attentive, not offensively physical.

While women appreciate men who demonstrate their attention and affection, most do not like to be fondled in public. Holding hands or putting your arm around her waist will probably be appreciated. More intimate caresses will probably not.

If days pass before you can pick up where you left off, stay in touch. Women's classic complaint about men is the heavy date followed by the heavy silence. Especially if things seemed to go well, she will wonder why you haven't maintained contact. Did she do something wrong? Did she miss some important cue? Did she just *think* you were both having a great time?

"When I don't hear from a guy, I go through a very bad and very predictable mental sequence," one woman told me. "First, I start making excuses for him—'Well, he's probably busy'—and then I go over and over our time together to see if there was something I did, or didn't do. Then I get really pissed off at him for not calling. *Then* I start feeling sorry for myself. At this point, even if he does call, it's almost too late. What I feel like saying is 'Why have you left me dangling, you son of a bitch?' It spoils whatever we had going for us, to put it mildly."

Of course, these days there is supposedly nothing to prevent a woman from doing the calling—except that what she is looking for is enough interest from you to take the initiative yourself.

So pick up the telephone. You may be waiting until you have another marvelous evening planned or because you are a little hesitant about where the relationship might take you, or simply out of shyness. Call anyway. Tell her where you are. Let her know you enjoyed the time you spent together. That's just good manners, after all. Include her in on what's been happening in your life since you saw her. Let her know when, or if, you might get together. Don't string her along, but don't assume you can maintain a connection with dead silence, either. Absence may make the heart grow fonder, but not under these circumstances.

If calling doesn't seem to fit, put pen to paper. Because so many people these days automatically reach for the telephone, personal letters have become rare and treasured objects, to be read and reread.

Start your own one-man campaign to revive the art of letter writing. Get some nice stationery—you can buy some good-looking note cards that don't require too many words to fill up—and write her a note: "I just wanted to let you know I can still smell the perfume you wore. Do you promise to wear it the next time?" (And don't be surprised if, later on, when she feels confident about you and your relationship, she takes you aside and shyly shows you a special box containing all the letters you ever wrote her, lovingly tied in . . . that's right, a blue ribbon.)

If you don't feel up to an original composition, send a card. From the romantic to the humorous, every drugstore in the country has a collection of "thinking of you" cards. Take some time to browse among them, and you will usually find one that reflects your sentiments.

When no means no

There are times when women—and men too, for that matter—really like the other person to take charge of deciding whether or not to make love. "Sometimes I honestly don't know if I feel like it or not," one woman said. "I like to be coaxed, persuaded. I think what it boils down to is when he shows me by persisting that he really, really wants to make love with me, his desire puts me in the mood."

This, of course, is the classic male dilemma: when does "no" mean "no," and when does it mean "I don't know" or "Not now, but keep trying," or "Yes, but you won't respect me if I don't say no at least once"?

When does it pay to persist, in other words, and when does persisting turn you into a pest? There is no single answer to this question that will apply at all times with all women, or even all times with one woman. As one woman put it, "Maybe it's a woman's lot, but it seems to me the guys I really want are the skittish ones, and the guys I don't want don't know when to give up."

To know which category you fit in, start by examining your own motivations. Are you trying to get her into bed because of your feelings for her or primarily to add another notch to your bedpost? Although most women can sense your intentions, making this distinction in your own mind may not always be easy. If you have been persisting with one woman for some time, the whole matter may have deteriorated to the level of a power struggle. If that's the case, you'd better chalk your "defeat" up to experience and call the whole thing off. (And if you find it hard to let go, you might want to ask yourself what you are getting out of such an obviously masochistic pursuit.)

There's an art to dealing with rejection without cutting a relationship off prematurely. Should you keep calling? Yes, up to a point. Let her know you are still interested in maintaining a friendship, but don't keep suggesting activities that are intended to culminate in bed. That approach is likely to result in failure for you and more unwanted pressure for her. Keep in mind that no one really likes to turn down another person, and if she feels this is what she has to look forward to, she will choose to avoid you entirely.

A point may come when you don't want to continue the relationship on these terms. If that happens, let her know. If she is still adamant, give up. There isn't much more you can do beyond this point.

On the other hand—and this is the hard part—don't give up too quickly. But don't go to the other extreme and get angry and insistent, either.

Instead, vary your approach. If at first you don't

succeed, try something else. It needn't be all or nothing. Whether you are actually in bed or simply on the phone trying to get a relationship started, if she says "no," then stop—but don't withdraw, actually or emotionally. Stop pushing and be alert to what she says or does next. You have proposed, she has disposed. Now the ball's in her court, so to speak. By her words and actions, she may let you know she wants to continue the preliminaries, if she is sure you will respect her wishes. If she isn't, she may want to stop altogether because she doesn't trust you not to push for more.

"The biggest problem I have with men may actually be with myself," a New England ski instructor said. "Making love is something I get into step by step. I like each step, but that doesn't always mean I want to go to the next one. Guys just assume if we get to step C, I'm automatically ready for the rest of the alphabet."

In fact, many, many women share this attitude. Keeping this fact in mind can reduce your share of "no's." There are times when women may be ready for physical closeness, but they do not want to make love. It's up to you to be sensitive enough to her needs to recognize the difference.

A good place to start is simply to become aware of the demands she faces in other parts of her life. Chances are these days the woman you are involved with has a career of her own which requires not only her time and physical energy but some psychic energy as well. If she's got to catch an early shuttle to Boston to close a deal the next morning, she may not be able to spend an evening making love, no matter how much she might want to under other circumstances.

Take her decision with good grace. Ask yourself what she would like. Time alone? A quick dinner that you prepare? She may like physical closeness—sleeping together, spending time in a hot tub, enjoying a massage—without sex. Men have a hard time accepting this distinction. They often assume that if they agree, they can manage to finagle intercourse sooner or later. Taking her at face value can pay off later, however. "One of the things I like best about my boyfriend is his enjoyment of just touching and being physically close without putting subtle pressure on me for something more," says a bookstore owner from Texas. "When I don't feel guilty or like I have to control him, I can just relax and enjoy the strength in his hands when he gives me a back rub, or the feel of his warmth next to me in bed."

Women also say no to being rushed into sex. You may have had a marvelous evening; every time she glanced at you through those long eyelashes you imagined what it would be like to peel her dress all the way off her milky-white shoulders. She may be feeling very romantic and caught up in the mood of the moment—reaching out to touch your face, smiling, leaning her head on your shoulder. That response in turn fuels your passion and convinces you that the next step is making love.

Wrong. She may simply be enjoying the anticipation, the romance, and the feeling of having all your attention and energy focused on appreciating her. Trying to hussle her into bed too soon destroys the mood and also raises the possibility in her mind that your interest in her is out of a simple need for sex.

When she turns you down in such a situation, back off—but not too far. It doesn't mean she wants you to go away, only that she doesn't want to be rushed into making love, just yet. "I hate it when a guy pushes too fast," one woman told me. "If I have to turn him down directly, he tends to get mad or get hurt. In either case, that lovely mood is broken, and nobody wins. He doesn't get what he wants, and neither do I."

One step at a time

The message is, then, if you're not sure whether she's ready for making love, don't force the issue or you're likely to get an answer she doesn't want to give and you don't want to get. Instead, slow down and give her some room for expressing herself—not necessarily verbally, but through her actions. Let's say you're sitting on the couch in her living room after a wonderful evening together. You have removed your jacket; she's kicked off her shoes. Lean toward her slowly, bringing your face close to hers. Look into eyes and kiss her gently near her mouth.

If she moves to bring her lips to yours, kiss her again, but don't rush or press. Let *her* quicken the pace. Don't embrace her yet. Simply experience the feeling of her lips against yours. "There's something incredibly sexy but also delicate and chaste about kissing when no other part of your bodies are touching," one young woman told me. "All sensation, every part of you gets focused on your mouth. It's a marvelous preview of things to come."

When a woman knows you are prepared to go slowly, she can let down her guard and allow herself to get physical in some truly creative ways. "I'll tell you something," a southern beauty once said to me. "There's nothing sexier for me than being with an attractive man who is willing to let me play with him without jumping right away into the main act. It's like having a gorgeous toy all to myself. I can run my fingers through his hair, unbutton his shirt, feel the muscles in his chest—it's a turn-on to play like that."

Look and listen

Focused on sex and filled with anxiety, some men and women talk too much at this stage. "I've had some strange experiences with men who can't stop talking," a Manhattan graphic artist told me. "We're touching and kissing, and he's carrying on a conversation about his business or the movie we just saw. It's like he's trying to distract me—or maybe himself—from what's going on."

Silences can often be sexier than words. "I love to be appreciated," a woman said. "If a man is kissing me and he murmurs something about my hair, or my skin, I love it. But sometimes it sounds more like a running commentary on the action. All that chatter destroys the mood."

So don't think that in order to show your feelings, you have to comment on everything that happens. Without words you can often attune yourself more closely to the physical and emotional sensations you—and she—are experiencing. Create some pregnant silences. Use your gaze and your body to maintain contact. Let your eyes show her the effect her closeness is having on you.

"Sometimes I walk up to my boyfriend, press myself against him, and lean back just a little to watch his face," a flight attendant said. "His eyes open wider, and I can see the pupils dilate. It happens every time. I love it."

What about when a woman talks too much? Usually, this is a sure sign that she's nervous. "I hate it when I do that," an L.A. physical therapist said. "I can hear my own voice as if someone else were talking who just will not stop."

In this situation, giving in to the temptation to say something like "Shut up and kiss me" probably won't get you very far. It might sound good in the movies, but in real life it will probably make her babble on even more frantically.

Instead, respond to the feeling underneath the words. Is there something you're trying to force her into that is upsetting her? Are you going too fast? Don't try to cut her off, but with your responses let her know that while you're listening to her words, you're also tuning in to her feelings. You don't have to mention them directly—this might only trigger a change of subject rather than the silence you both really want—but you can act on them. Slow down. Give her some room to relax and feel comfortable.

Good kissing

Kisses are emotional fingerprints; no two people's are exactly the same. How you kiss reveals a lot about the kind of person you are and how you relate to women.

We do a lot of kissing that is more like a handshake than a preamble to lovemaking. Even these social kisses reveal a lot, at least according to the creative director of a small Los Angeles ad agency. "You know the A-frame kiss?" she asked. "The one where the upper bodies come together but a safe distance is maintained below the belt? Then there's the tropical-fish kiss, where the lips are pursed and hard and sort of stuck out to keep the other person at lip's length, so to speak. These kissers are terribly appropriate, but a little uptight emotionally. Then there's the sneaky social kisser. He sort of insinuates a little extra pressure, or tries to get some lip action going, but he never says anything or declares himself. There's something sort of pathetic about someone who uses that approach.

"My favorite social kisser combines heartiness with sensitivity. How can I describe it? He smiles and hugs you and gives you a big, friendly kiss. It's not overbearing, just sort of firm and soft at the same time. You can tell this kind of person enjoys people, likes you, and can use his body to express himself."

What about when kissing means more than "Hello, I'm glad to see you?" The women I talked to were unanimous on what they wanted: responsiveness and tenderness.

"Sometimes I like to be overpowered," one woman said, "but I also like room to kiss back. Most men move in too fast, especially for the first real kiss. One minute we're embracing, and the next he's pushing my face in and mauling my mouth. The only sensation I feel is pressure. It can actually be a little frightening."

Remember that the lips are among the most sensitive parts of the body. Brushing your lips lightly against hers can produce an exquisite sensation of smoothness and warmth. With the slightest increase in pressure you can feel the softness of her lips and sense behind the softness a corresponding pressure from her that tells you she is responding.

Proceed in small steps. Kiss the corners of her mouth. Take her lower lip lightly between yours. Don't try any suction, yet.

"Little kisses," one woman told me, "drive me crazy. It's a kind of delicious tease when a man kisses me on the mouth, and then nibbles my lower lip, and then kisses me again on the corner of my mouth. I can stand it for just a few seconds, and then I want to devour him."

Vary your technique. Alternate pressure with lightness. Prolonged heavy kissing can make the lips numb and even sore. Use your lips to trace the contours of her face. Feel the delicate movements of her eyelids under your lips. Etch the lines of her cheek and discover the hollow where jaw, ear, and neck meet. Allow your breath to brush softly across her skin. Take her earlobe gently between your lips.

"It's true what they say about ears," a blond gallery owner told me. "When a man blows in my ear, or runs his tongue around the outside, I can *hear* it. I can feel it in my *knees*. It just shuts out every other sensation."

Open-mouth kissing, and especially deep penetration of the tongue, represents a level of intimacy that women do not like to be rushed into. "When I'm ready, it's wonderful, a real sense of merging with the other person," one woman reported, "but if I'm not, it feels like being violated, smothered."

"Some men will sort of grab your tongue with their teeth and suck on it, hard," another woman complained, "and it hurts. I get the feeling they're trying to prove something."

Instead of forcing her, try to sense her readiness. Kiss her with your lips slightly open. If she opens her lips, extend your tongue slightly. Run it gently across her lower lip. Allow her tongue to explore your mouth without overpowering her with yours. If she seems hesitant, don't push. When she is ready, she will let you know.

One young man, barely out of his teens, had some words of wisdom that went far beyond his years. "Always let her do the escalating. For example, if you're kissing, you've got to sense exactly the moment when her kissing becomes more passionate, and only then move in with more. Later on, there's time for you to take off, but at this point, you want to give her the chance to make her own choice. Letting her do this will pay off later for both of you."

Breasts

A woman's breasts are sources of visual and tactile erotic pleasure for you, and for her they are symbols of her femininity in the broadest meaning of the word—all the way from motherhood to her sense of herself as a sexually attractive woman. They are also directly connected to the sources of her genital excitation. "When a man caresses my breasts the way I like it," a Los Angeles model said, "I feel it right between my legs."

The major complaint women make is that men assume this direct connection is a fairly short road, one which they travel too quickly, too roughly, and too predictably. As one woman lamented, "Most guys seem to be following a procedure they all learned in the same locker room: you know, two minutes of hands outside the bra, one minute of bare tit, a couple of sucks on the nipple, and then bam! Grab for the crotch."

Rough handling of the breasts is a turnoff for all women. "I have real problems with this either-or situation many men get into," a woman told me. "They seem to think that either it's hands off totally, or else it's no holds barred. I hate to be grabbed and squeezed. How would a man like to have his balls treated that way?"

If you keep in mind that what you are doing is *appreciating* her breasts and not copping a feel or pushing her buttons, you can create profound sexual pleasure for her—and for yourself as well.

Instead of grabbing for a breast at the first opportunity, orchestrate a sexual crescendo. Run your hands down her sides. Allow your hands to brush against the undercurve of her breasts, lightly. Cup them gently and pause to let her feel the warmth of your hands. Kiss her in the hollow of her neck and with your tongue make a slow path down to a spot between her breasts. Trace the line where the cushion of her breasts meets the firmer surface of her chest.

One of the most erotic sensations for many women is having a man's head buried in their breasts. "It makes me feel incredibly sexy and desirable," one woman claimed. "There are just so many sensations. I can feel his lips, the weight of his head, his breath, and his hair brushing against my skin. And if he says something or sort of growls, his voice reverberates all through my body."

Another woman reported something her boyfriend

did the first time they made love that she found irresistible. "He put his lips between my breasts just where my blouse buttoned, and moved them down as he unbuttoned each button. Then he opened my blouse and unhooked my bra. I felt this sudden rush of cold air on my skin. It made me feel terribly exposed and vulnerable, but before I could do anything he covered one breast with his hand, and took the other in his mouth, and the cold went way. That sudden warm feeling just melted me."

If a woman is at all self-conscious about her breasts, she may be most comfortable lying back. Gently massage them with the palms of your hands, applying pressure from the base toward the nipple. With your tongue and lips make smaller and smaller circles, working toward the nipple, but not touching it yet. Go back and forth from one breast to the other, pushing them together tenderly to create a crevice you can explore with your tongue.

As she becomes more aroused she may twist her body to bring her nipple to your mouth. Take it gently between your lips and kiss it, wetting the rosy area around it. A woman's nipples are incredibly sensitive at this point, and any rough treatment or painful friction from your dry hands can hurt her. "I like a man to touch my breasts with his hands, but when my nipples are erect they are so sensitive his hand can hurt too much," said one woman. "I prefer the smooth wetness and warmth of his mouth, with gentle suction, and his tongue moving back and forth across the nipple."

Some women like very gentle bites on the nipple with your teeth—*if* they're very gentle. "It's an exquisite feeling," one woman reported, "just at the edge of pain, but not quite. It takes a very sensitive man to do it right for me."

If your partner is not self-conscious about her breasts, you may want to try something a friend of mine likes to do. "My girlfriend likes her breasts, and she loves to watch the effect they have on me. I ask her to move around—sit up, lie on her side, let them fall over my face. Each way they look different. I like to lie on my back with my hands behind my head and have her move them over me back and forth, with the nipples just grazing first my chest and then my mouth. I get so hard it hurts, and she says she gets off on how carried away I get."

Disrobing

To engage in these kinds of erotic encounters assumes nakedness, which in turn assumes that at some point both of you have removed your clothes. In some cases, the momentum of sexual passion will take you through disrobing without your even being aware of the process. In other cases, however, disrobing is a big issue—for some women, an act tantamount to having sex, and for everyone, an awkward and passion-chilling confusion of snaps, hooks, buttons, and zippers.

When and how to disrobe is best left to the particular circumstances of time and place and the preferences of you and your partner. I talked to one woman who had just had a fantastic weekend with a man that began by her disrobing him. "I was sitting at the edge of the bed, and he was standing in front of me. I unbuttoned his shirt, and stripped it off his shoulders," she said with relish. "Then I unbuckled his belt, unhooked his pants, and slowly slid them down his leg. I looked up at his face the whole time, so that I could see his reaction. I felt dominant and submissive at the same time."

Many women like to be undressed by the man; ideally, they see each removal of a garment as an opportunity to be appreciated, but the reality is that as each garment comes off they can often feel more exposed and unsure of their physical appearance.

To work toward the ideal, start by making sure the lighting is flattering and warm. Candles cast the

rosiest, warmest glow, but in their absence a low
light will do. Don't inspect; appreciate. Maintain
physical contact. Share your excitement and sexual
arousal with her; let her know, in other words, that
she turns you on.

If your partner resists total nudity, don't insist—or
despair. There may be some hidden benefits for you.
Although the classic picture of two lovers entwined
does not include clothes, some shy couples have found
that by keeping a few clothes on, they feel less
inhibited.

Said one self-conscious woman, "I tried to get comfortable with being totally naked because I thought
my boyfriend wanted it, and because I thought that's
what you're supposed to do. But I can't help it—when
I'm not wearing anything I feel so self-conscious I
can't think about anything else. So I always keep
something on, even if it's an open kimono or a blouse.
It doesn't get in the way of things half as much as my
nervousness did. Now I can really enjoy myself."

If you sense reluctance from your partner, you might
want to borrow a page from the sex therapists' book.
One of their prescriptions for couples with sexual
problems is to ask them to disrobe and go to bed but
to promise not to make love. Their purpose is to
remove the worrisome focus on sexual intercourse by
encouraging people to take the time to get comfortable with the stage of physical intimacy preceding
intercourse itself.

For this to work, you have to mean it. It may
require some self-control to lie naked in the same
bed with a woman you find physically attractive, but
not so much as you may think. Even if you have an
erection, nowhere but in high-school sex lore is it
written that you must do anything about it. If you
can shift your interest from "getting your rocks off"
to building intimacy step by step with your partner,
you will be setting the stage for far more fulfilling
sexual experiences at a later time when she feels like
responding in kind.

Many women are susceptible to guilt trips men lay on them about the power of masculine sexual needs and the opinion men have of women who tease and then don't come through. It never occurs to many of these women that they can ask for physical closeness before they may be ready to make love. Yet that is exactly what many of them want.

"I know women take longer generally in the area of sex," one woman told me with some hesitation. "I know there have been times when I really wanted to be with a man—in bed, even—without having sex with him, yet. But I always assumed this was not fair to men, that I would be leading them on, or that they would agree but then try something funny. I just thought this wasn't how the game was played."

Men who go along with a woman's needs to take it slowly report benefits that other men might find surprising. "You discover a whole new world of touch that isn't explicitly sexual but is very enjoyable," one man told me. "And, let's face it, sometimes it's a relief for the man too. I know the first time I make love with a woman isn't always perfect. I'm nervous, and she's nervous, and there's an element of doing it because it's expected. Taking it in stages can be better.

"Also, you earn her respect and trust, so that when you do get to the point when you're both ready to make love, she really feels free to let go, because she trusts you."

Discovering her point of no return

When it comes to deciding whether or not to make love with a man, especially for the first time, most women have their own point of no return.

For some, it is deep kissing. For others, it may be allowing their breasts to be fondled. For many, it is the act of disrobing. "I would never take my clothes off in a man's presence," their thinking goes, "if I didn't want to make love with him."

Accomplished lovers realize the importance of recognizing just when a woman is aroused to this point. Until she is, your efforts to proceed further will be fruitless, and in fact may turn her off so completely you will never have another chance.

Not that women don't sometimes make love without being fully aroused. I talked to women who spoke of making love under these circumstances as a gift they gave freely to the man they loved. "There are times when I know the red lights simply aren't going to go on for me," one admitted, "but I still can enjoy the experience—as long as I don't feel pressure to fake it. Of course, you've got to realize we know each other pretty well by now."

Pressure is exactly what you want to avoid, especially if you and your partner are just embarking on an intimate relationship. You may be able to manipulate her into having sex with you, but that's what it will be—having sex, no more—and the resentment and disappointment she may feel as a result could poison the rest of your relationship.

You don't have to be a mind reader to avoid this state of affairs. The key is to *go slowly* and give her the chance to stop at any point without feeling guilty or inadequate. You may have reached a point of such sexual excitement that all you can think of is unwrapping her like a lovely Christmas present. Remember, though, that this may be a bigger step for her, one that she doesn't want to rush into until she feels ready.

CHAPTER SIX

Foreplay

If today's man knows nothing else about making love to women, he knows about the importance of foreplay. Foreplay, he has been told, is what separates the men from the slam-bam boys. A knowledge of foreplay "technique" marks a man as an accomplished lover of women, one who can play them like a violin and make them vibrate for hours.

Furthermore, he knows that the essential ingredient of foreplay is time—time for the woman to get relaxed, time for her to get in the mood, time for her to experience the first of all the orgasms she's going to have. Of course, knowing it takes women longer than men to reach orgasm, he's got to get her up to speed before he really enters the race, so to speak, so that they can both cross the finish line at roughly the same time.

Yet among all the women I talked to, it was men's performance in the area of foreplay that earned the loudest groans and generated the most anger and disappointment.

Maggie's response was typical. "I am so tired of these lovers with mental checklists!" she wailed. "You know, a minute on the earlobe, two minutes on each breast, kiss-kiss-moan, and then down to business. It's not the speed, it's the impersonality that gets me."

"My boyfriend watches me like a hawk when we first start to make love," one dissatisfied woman said. "As soon as I express any kind of pleasure, that's it for foreplay, as far as he's concerned, and away we go. It's inhibiting, to put it mildly."

Women resent being thought of as cars that need to be warmed up before they can be driven. Nor do they appreciate guilt trips. "I had a lover once who fancied himself quite the expert," a Manhattan attorney told me. "While he was caressing my breasts or stroking me between the legs, he'd say, 'I'm doing this just for you, you know.' I guess I was supposed to be grateful, but what I felt was guilty for making him work so hard."

The "play" in foreplay

No matter how many articles on women's sexual needs you read or how accomplished a sexual technician you become, you will never make love to women the way they want to be made love to if you fail to understand a very basic male-female difference.

Men equate making love with intercourse. Any preliminaries, therefore, are exactly that: warm-ups before the Main Event. This attitude affects their technique, their timing, and their expectations both for themselves and their partners.

Women, on the other hand, have a more expansive definition of making love. It includes intercourse, certainly, but it does not exclude everything that goes before. Even the word "before" bespeaks a masculine point of view. As one woman tried to explain to me, "When I'm in bed with a man and feel sexy and erotic, almost everything we do together is making love, as far as I'm concerned. Sometimes, I don't even want to have intercourse, because that means we're close to the end."

Men have a very hard time believing such statements. They tend to hear them as women's attempts to be understanding about failed erections and other masculine performance problems. As my friend Ferd put it, "Yeah, yeah, that's what they *say*, but what they *mean* is that it's okay if you don't deliver all the time. Well, I appreciate the understanding, but I'd rather deliver, and I bet they'd rather I did too."

Ironically, you stand the best chance of "delivering," in Ferd's sense of the word, if you can forget about it. Instead of considering foreplay as preliminary to intercourse, think of it as an end in itself. You may have to break through some cultural conditioning about what men "should" do and expect in bed to arrive at this new point of view. The payoff, however, can be incredibly expanded sensuous experiences in which you benefit just as much as your partner.

Nongenital techniques of arousal

Once you decide to focus on the "play" in foreplay, you may discover your repetoire of things to do is rather inadequate. You may have learned a few techniques for turning a woman on, but setting up an extended sensuous experience calls for real creativity and imagination.

Start with the fact that women can be sexually aroused by a variety of nongenital activities. The important ingredients here are touch, warmth, scent, lighting—and caring.

Baths and showers

Warm water can be a marvelously sensual medium for establishing physical contact, especially if you and your partner are about to make love for the first time.

One of today's most potent fantasies, of course, is a hot tub under the stars, with the surf pounding in the background and wisps of fog mingling with steam rising from the water's surface. "When you're outdoors in a hot tub on a cool evening, you've got that wonderful contrast between the cool air and the hot water," said Angela, a Marin County social worker lucky enough to know. "It creates a special world for just you and your lover. You can sit and look at the stars, and sip a glass of white wine, and snuggle down in the water when you get cold."

In a hot tub nudity is less of a major statement; there's an almost playful quality about it that appeals to women who might be otherwise very self-conscious about removing their clothes.

Says Jeff, a Sausalito architect who recently built a hot tub outside his bedroom, "You can wrap a towel around yourself and take it off at the last minute before you jump in. Once you're in you can get used to being naked without feeling you're on display. And you can touch feet or embrace and just sort of fool around without getting too heavy right away. It reminds me a little of playing in the water as a kid, except that you're alone with a lovely woman and neither of you are wearing anything."

Caressing each other under water adds a dimension of sensuality not possible on dry land. Skin feels smoother and is more responsive to the touch. The water buoys up your body to some extent; the weightlessness you feel can transport you and your partner into a world where abandoning your inhibitions and literally "going with the flow" becomes almost automatic.

"Being in a hot tub with my lover is like being in a warm, protected cocoon," Angela said. "I can't always tell where the water stops and our bodies begin. When I close my eyes, everything disappears but the physical sensations. It really is the ultimate."

Of course, not everyone has access to the ultimate. Most people do have tubs or showers, however, and these too can become bowers of sensual delights. In a tub or shower, you can use scented soaps to lather each other up and get slippery-sexy.

Mark, an ingenious novelist, likes to begin an evening of lovemaking with an extended shower for two in his bathroom, which he lights with several votive candles. "The bathroom's pretty much a dump and the shower isn't big," he admits, "but the candlelight hides a lot. We get in and soap each other down, starting with the back and legs and then slithering into the better places. The candlelight makes anyone look beautiful and sexy. I get so turned on I can't touch my cock for fear I'll come too soon."

Marcia, a busy buyer with career demands that often wear her down by the end of the day, swears by the restorative hot bath. "Jim sets it up for me—he draws the water, puts in some special scented oil he knows I like, and then ushers me in. Usually he's taken off his clothes. When I get in, he kneels by the tub and starts rubbing my shoulders, slowly, without saying anything. It's hypnotic. I can feel all my worries float away. Just when I'm about to drop off, I notice his rhythm change, and he starts working his hands down to my breasts, which he strokes and massages slowly and gently. The oil in the water makes his hands slippery. Sometimes he'll start with my foot, and massage each of my toes, one by one—who would think toes could be that sexy?—and then move up my leg to gently stroke my inner thigh but nothing else. After half an hour, I'm usually in a wonderful state halfway between sleep and being turned on. Whatever happens after that is gravy."

The sexy massage

For those who would rather stay dry and in bed, there is the sexy massage. You don't have to be a professional masseur to make this an incredibly erotic event. In fact, amateur attempts at so-called "therapeutic" massages that involve pounding, pummeling, and "working out the blocks" can not only be very nonsexy but painful and even dangerous.

A massage requires some advance planning. Visit your local emporium and check out the availability of scented oils. Some have ingredients that provide added warmth when applied to the skin. Be sure whatever you buy tastes good, because where your hands have been, your tongue and lips are likely to follow.

Take some time to set the stage. Is your bed linen clean and fresh? Have you arranged soft and sexy lighting? Candles never fail, although a red light bulb also casts a rosy and sensuous glow, and a red scarf draped over a lampshade creates the same effect. Background music can add to the mood, especially if you select the kind of music you know she likes. Incidentally, if you have a fireplace, you may want to consider setting up a towel and some soft pillows in front of it. There is nothing sexier than the warmth of a fire, the dancing flames that cast a primal and lovely erotic light on your bodies, and the delightfully forbidden aspect of carrying on on the floor.

While some women may enjoy making love all oily and slippery, many others will worry about messy sheets. You may want to spread an oversized beach towel on the bed that you can remove later. (Depending on the mood of the moment, you may also want to arrange for a bath or shower after the massage and before making love.)

The purpose of all this advance planning is to create a special world for just the two of you, out of time and place.

Begin slowly. Your partner is lying comfortably on her stomach. Knead her shoulders and neck gently but firmly. Get into a slow even rhythm as you gradually expand your movements to include her upper back and sides. Feel the fragile juncture where her upper and lower body meet.

Then shift to her feet. Lift each one and massage the arch, the instep, and each toe. Slide your cupped hand along her calf to the back of her knee. Move your hands up her thighs, sensing how the skin becomes softer and finer there.

To escalate to the next level, caress her inner thighs with each thumb. If she is ready to proceed, she will move her legs apart. Don't rush ahead, though. The important thing at this point is to keep the rhythm slow and even. "When my boyfriend is giving me a slow massage, I start out feeling sort of excited and a little turned on," a dancer told me, "and then I move into deep relaxation. After fifteen or twenty minutes I start getting really aroused, but differently from the first time. It feels like waves just starting to crash on the beach."

When she has relaxed completely and is ready for more, turn her over on her back. She may have been lost in her own fantasies, so greet her with a kiss. Remember that in this position she may feel more vulnerable. Ask her to shut her eyes so that she can concentrate on the physical sensation of your warm, slippery hands on her shoulders and breasts. This time use lighter, softer motions. Make circles with your palms around the base of her breasts and in the hollows and creases that form at their base and sides. Gently push her breasts upward to create cleavage. Lightly tongue each nipple and the surrounding aureoles. Repeat the process several times, using the same hypnotic rhythm.

Slowly, with just enough pressure to make contact, move your fingertips down to her stomach and abdomen. Trace gentle concentric circles, featherlight, smaller and smaller until you reach her navel.

For some women—and men too—navels are very sensitive erogenous zones. "When a man sticks his tongue in my navel," one woman admitted to me, "it's a deep and powerful feeling, a kind of electric tickling. I don't like too much all the time, but one unexpected thrust of his tongue can send me over the edge."

As you near her genital area be sure not to increase your pace or speed up the rhythm. Allow your fingers to brush lightly across her public hair as you massage her inner thighs and the crease where her thighs join her torso. If she spreads her legs and offers her genitals up to your hands, softly stroke the outer lips with your thumbs, but don't apply too much pressure.

Move down to her legs. At this point you may want

to replace your hands with your tongue. In fact, many longtime lovers like to vary the experience by occasionally giving their partner a massage using only their tongue and lips (or a feather or a silk scarf). With your tongue, you can attend to some of her less-known erogenous zones, like the back of the knee, the inner elbow, and the instep. Said one responsive young woman, "When my lover kisses and licks the back of my knee long enough, I can go crazy. Sometimes I can almost come."

As you move your lips down her inner thigh leave your hand on her genitals. Allow her movements to tell you where she wants to feel it and how much pressure she wants.

Turnabout is fun

One of the biggest turn-ons women can experience is to know that they are turning *you* on. As you massage her you can let her know the effect she is having on you—by sighs or smiles or an occasional "Boy, do you feel good."

Or, why not have her give *you* a massage? Many men feel uncomfortable being on the receiving end—passivity is not part of our masculine conditioning—but it can be a wonderful experience. "I get tired of always being the one who 'does,'" says Ted, a high-powered San Francisco attorney. "Sometimes I like being 'done to.' It's a relief to have someone else take charge—and it's incredibly sexy when the woman has some imagination and feels free to express it. It's like a gift she's giving me."

Women, for their part, love being turned loose to play with a male body they find attractive. "When I give my lover a massage, I think of it as the feminine equivalent of looking at *Playboy*," one woman said. "I just love knowing that he's all mine, and I can feel and stroke and play with whatever I want. Sometimes my boyfriend will just flop back on the bed, give me a really sexy look, and say, 'All right, woman, do with me what you will.' I've always wanted someone who would let me do that."

If you're the highly excitable type and don't want to spoil the fun too soon, you may want to establish some ground rules, like no extended touching of your genitals. Otherwise, just relax and enjoy it. More important, let her *know* that you're enjoying it. Words can help—"My God, that feels so incredibly wonderful!" —but again, don't feel you have to engage in a running commentary. If what she's doing makes you feel like moaning, moan. She'll love the feeling of power, and by not holding back you'll loosen up and feel more. Don't be shy about body movements— arching your back, squirming, thrusting. Getting into your feelings physically can increase the power and intensity of your orgasm later on.

If you think you're about to lose control, ask her to stop for a while until you feel like continuing. The whole idea is not to rush to orgasm but to make this part of lovemaking intense and long-lasting enough to give you both time to become totally and equally aroused.

Deep kissing

As you might expect, the French have a word for it: *maraichinage*, the long, languorous kisses in which your tongues explore the insides of each other's mouths at leisure. This kind of kissing goes beyond the quick thrusting penetration of what we called "French kissing" in high school. Deep kissing is open and wet, slow as well as fast, gentle as well as insistent. "It's like having intercourse for me," I was told by a teacher in her thirties. "I feel totally open and receptive. I run my tongue across his teeth and tongue, and the roof of his mouth, and he is doing the same thing to me. Sometimes I tease him by trying to capture his tongue and suck on it. Sometimes I let him explore me. Sometimes we just lie there with our mouths together, not moving much at all."

How long is enough foreplay? A recent survey among women indicated that most preferred at least thirty minutes before being ready for intercourse itself. Better than any clock watching, however, is your sensitivity to your partner's readiness. If you have given her the message that she can set the pace, she will let you know when she is ready by reaching out to you.

If you have been able to shift the focus from the Main Event to the experiences and sensations of the moment, you may be surprised to discover that—like your partner—you may want to extend this period as long as possible yourself. As one woman summed it up, "A sensitive lover knows how to initiate as well as to lie back and let it happen. The feelings just build and build, but always with a kind of tantalizing holding back. After a while, I get so aroused I'm just begging for it."

CHAPTER SEVEN

Lovemaking à la Carte

Despite the so-called sexual revolution, most of us are still shy about sexual experimentation. Old teachings die hard, even among the most liberated. Isn't what we're doing a little . . . well, kinky? Unhygienic? Harmful? Immoral—or, worse, self-centered?

As a man, you might be surprised to learn that women have made great progress in overcoming these taboos—more, in fact, than many men. Spurred by the move to "take charge of their bodies," many women have explored various means of sexual gratification—including masturbation and oral sex either in practice or in their fantasies. They have discovered that a lot of what their mothers warned them against (or never even mentioned) *feels good*—often better, in fact, than intercourse itself.

In talking to these women, I discovered that many of them consider this information to be their little secret, best kept from the men in their lives. "Let's face it," one said. "Men are terribly threatened to find out women can pleasure themselves. It makes them feel unnecessary and inadequate."

Added another: "It's one thing to bring yourself to orgasm in the privacy of your bedroom. I love that feeling of total abandon, without having to worry about who I'm with or what I'm doing or how I look. But with a man? I'd like to. I mean, that would be the ultimate. But I'd feel . . . I don't know, inhibited, weird."

Giving each other permission

Rose is typical of a lot of women who, having made a conscious effort to expand their sexual horizons, are now looking for men to match them. Her sexual awareness came as a result of her participation in a local women's group. Growing up in a traditional Italian Catholic family, she never would have thought the day would come when she would sit around with a group of women inspecting each other's genitals. Yet that is exactly what happened.

"It was part of a workshop for preorgasmic women," she said, "and the idea was to desensitize any negative feelings you had about yourself, and to learn more about your own anatomy. We also had homework assignments on masturbating. I know it sounds strange, but I found out so many things about how to pleasure myself, and what I like to do in bed. It had never occurred to me before that there were so many possibilities, or that I even had a choice. But I know now, and I want the man in my life to know too."

You are going to be meeting more and more women with Rose's enlightened attitudes, women who know what they want and are not afraid to insist on it. And what they want far exceeds the standard lovemaking menu.

There's no reason for you to deny yourself or your partner the heightened pleasure that can come from blending some nonstandard practices into your mutual lovemaking. It's all a matter, first, of getting your own head straight and then creating an environment in which you both feel free to throw your hesitations to the wind and lose yourselves in exquisite inventiveness.

First, consider your own reactions. If you're like most men, you are probably not exactly thrilled to read studies showing that many women can achieve better and more frequent orgasms through means other than the old in-out.

Arnie, a friend of mine who had always considered himself fairly liberated, had to change his way of thinking, but now he has the right idea. "Last summer my girlfriend and I went camping," he said, "and the first night when we were in the tent she started playing with herself. I sort of moved in to take over, but she told me to just watch her. So I did, but I felt really stupid. Part of me was turned on, but another part felt sort of useless. She got turned on like she never had before, though, and when we made love about ten minutes later, it was better than it had ever been. She said the same thing.

"First, I thought, why hadn't I ever been able to do that to her? But then I thought, what difference does it make? It really brought us to a whole new level. Now we often masturbate ourselves before we make love."

Once you let go of the "there must be something wrong with me" attitude, you can begin to consider all the exciting turn-ons an expanded sexual menu makes possible—like the one I was told about by a flight attendant based in San Francisco.

"I love to lie on the bed and massage myself with olive oil," she said. "My boyfriend lies next to me, but he's not allowed to touch me. I start with my breasts and my nipples. Eventually I get around to putting my hands between my legs, and I start stroking myself, and rubbing my clitoris. I can do it just like I like it, slow and easy.

"But the sexiest part is watching him watching me. I never take my eyes off his. I'm turning myself on and him too. When he can't stand it anymore, he enters me, and boy, am I ready!"

And as Arnie will tell you, for those who pay attention there's an added benefit to this whole process. "By watching her, I find out what she really likes—you know, the rhythm, and where to touch, and how long. It's great knowing just how to turn her on."

Mutual masturbation

If you would like to participate more directly in the action, try masturbating at the same time she does. Many people are put off by this kind of disconnected "being alone together," as a friend of mine calls it. Also, for many men the act of masturbating in the presence of a woman calls up memories of trying to work a dead penis back to life. But studies show that both men and women can stimulate themselves more efficiently (if that word can be applied to making love) and effectively than others can. After all, who knows your body better than you?

Besides, it can be a turn-on for your partner. "The first time my lover masturbated in my presence, it felt like a gift of intimacy," one woman wrote. "It's such a private thing to share, more private than intercourse, really. I felt very close to him."

Or you can masturbate each other. The phrase itself may sound awkward, but the experience can be powerfully erotic for both of you, and especially for your partner.

To understand why, you need to know something about the differences between male and female anatomy. During intercourse, the penis receives direct stimulation from the vagina on the glans, or head, where its most sensitive nerves are located. These nerves, in women, are located in the clitoris, which feels like a tiny button at the top of a woman's inner vaginal lips. During intercourse it is likely to receive only indirect stimulation. Without proper positioning, therefore, the woman may not receive enough direct stimulation during intercourse itself to reach orgasm.

Manually stimulating your partner calls for sensitivity to and awareness of her needs and preferences. Some women prefer gentle but direct stimulation of the sensitive clitoris. Others, for whom direct stimulation is too painful, prefer rubbing of the entire genital area with increasing attention given to the lips.

Start with the heel of your hand toward her navel, resting on her pubic bone. Massage the entire genital area; take your cue for how much pressure she likes from how hard she pushes back. With your middle finger, part her outer lips and probe gently for her vaginal opening. Softly trace her inner lips, maintaining some pressure on her pubic bone.

As she becomes aroused you can feel her clitoris become engorged and hard. Touch it gently. Be sure your finger is moist—either with oil, lubricants from her vagina, or your own saliva. If this is the first time, allow her body movements to tell you if it's too sensitive and where she wants stimulation, and how much. Try putting her hand over yours so that she can guide you. There's nothing wrong with asking her directly, of course, but for many people such direct "how to" communication can spoil the mood, especially if the relationship is a new one.

Alternate the stroking of her clitoral area with other stimulation. Insert your fingers in her vagina. Take her nipple in your mouth and suck it with increasing pressure. Your multiple attentions to her pleasure zones can have a devastating effect. "I love that three-ring-circus feeling," purred an actress from L.A. "The sensations are so intense I really can't tell where they're coming from. That's when I feel like screaming."

Some women are not comfortable with mutual masturbation when they are first getting to know a man—not because they don't enjoy the physical sensations, but because they don't want to appear "brazen." As one woman admitted, "I know women are supposed to take responsibility for their own orgasms and all that, but until I know a man well—get to trust him, I guess—I really don't like to expose myself that way."

Liza, recently divorced, decided to treat the whole question of masturbation as a research project and read everything she could find on the subject. Then she started practicing—on herself and her new lover—and now she considers herself an expert.

"I *love* to stroke his penis and watch it grow in my hands while he's playing with me," she said. "I start with my fingers wrapped around the base and move them up toward the head, tugging just a little. Or I'll flutter my fingers on the underside of the shaft. Oil is good, because it makes a kind of sexy slipperiness he likes.

"Occasionally masturbation is a substitute for intercourse, but more often it's a first course. Sometimes we'll be lying in bed, too tired or whatever, and we'll just start playing around with each other. Pretty soon, we get each other so hot we aren't too tired anymore."

Oral sex

Ask any woman: if fingers are good, tongues and lips are better. They're warmer, wetter, softer, and capable of a wider and more intense range of pleasure giving, from teasingly soft and subtle to hard-driving and insistent, than either fingers or (brace yourself) penises.

According to findings in *The Cosmo Report*, 84 percent of all women surveyed regularly participate in both fellatio and cunnilingus. At the same time, many women have some deep-seated reservations about oral sex—on both the giving and receiving ends. To be a sensitive lover, you need to be aware of what these are before you can concentrate on "doing it right."

Fellatio

Some women will suck a man's penis as an almost automatic manipulation to which they don't give much thought and from which they derive little pleasure ("Sometimes it's the only way he can get hard").

For most women, however, it's a gift of love they give themselves and their lovers—a level of intimacy they reserve for those they trust and feel close to. "When I take his soft penis in my mouth, he feels so vulnerable I just melt," one woman confided. "And when I feel it grow, I imagine what it will be like inside me."

"Trust" is the operative word here, especially for the inexperienced. One of the major reservations women have about performing fellatio—also known as "going down," "giving head," and giving a "blow job"—is losing control and choking. This fear may have been engendered by *Deep Throat*, the film that did so much to educate the public about the practice in the first place. As one young woman admitted, "I never saw the movie, but from hearing about it I always assumed that there was some kind of anatomical contortion you had to master, sort of like sword swallowing."

Another fear is having to swallow a man's ejaculate. For some women, this takes time to work up to. Others never become comfortable with the idea.

"My squeamishness over swallowing his semen really surprised my lover," said an East Coast public-TV producer. "Maybe because of my work, he assumed a degree of sophistication I just didn't have, certainly not in this area. I'd read enough about it, God knows, but I didn't know what it would feel or taste like. And the last thing I wanted to risk was gagging or throwing up."

"It's the 'spit or swallow' issue," another woman said, "a very hot topic in women's locker rooms all across the country, I can tell you. It's a very personal thing, and I think it's got more to do with the individual woman than with her feelings for her lover."

Said a third: "Oral sex is definitely *the* sign of sexual sophistication these days. But it goes against so much of what women have been taught in the past that they really need help. One of the things that helped me was tasting my boyfriend's semen, just a little bit, before we ever tried oral sex. It was sort of salty, and there wasn't nearly as much as I had feared."

If your girlfriend has some qualms about oral sex in general, or swallowing in particular, you won't get very far by taking her reluctance personally. Adopting a "you would if you loved me" attitude misses the point completely and is likely to produce a totally unnecessary power struggle. You will find it far more rewarding to look at the whole matter as she might see it—frightening because it is unfamiliar and because it violates some ingrained cultural dictates that may be more powerful than she had thought.

The answer, obviously, is to go slowly and make sure she knows she can set the pace every step of the way. Let her know how pleasurable the sensation of her lips on the head of your penis can be, or the combination of her tongue and fluttery fingers running up and down the shaft. If and when she takes your penis in her mouth, don't ram it down her throat. Practice a little restraint; in the process, you may discover some marvelous sensations that you can keep going longer than you may think possible.

And needless to say, don't ejaculate in her mouth without warning. Give her the choice of stopping first. If self-control is going to be a problem, you might try using a condom. It may not feel (or taste) so good, but it will avoid the problem for both of you.

Cunnilingus

As every experienced lover knows, the best way to interest a woman in performing fellatio is to perform cunnilingus on her. Ironically, considering its popularity among women, this is one aspect of making love where most men are very uninformed, either from some unadmitted squeamishness or just simple ignorance.

For one thing, although each succeeding survey on

sexual habits shows more and more women interested in cunnilingus, they are very reluctant to insist—or even suggest—that their lovers perform it. Their hesitation stems from fears about their genital odor and taste. "Women are bombarded from all sides with advertisements for vaginal deodorants, deodorant tampons, scented douches, and sprays," says a New York sex therapist. "No wonder they get the message that they're dirty 'down there.'"

The first thing you should do, therefore, is to reassure your partner that she tastes and smells just fine. To allay her fears (and yours too, perhaps) you might want to bathe together first, to make sure both of you are fresh and clean. By taking the opportunity to let her know that you like her scent, you will remove any lingering worries she may have that could get in the way of her enjoyment.

With these concerns laid to rest, you can begin. If you've got a reasonably full head of hair, you might be interested in a report I got from a woman in Chicago. "My lover has beautiful, longish red hair, very thick," she told me. "Before he goes down on me, he always sort of tickles me between my legs with his hair. That's the sign, and I immediately feel the anticipation building. It feels like feathers. Very sexy."

Start with kissing her abdomen and inner thighs (especially the crease where thigh joins torso) and then proceed to the genital area itself. With your thumbs, gently part the labia and kiss them, inserting your tongue. Move up to the clitoral shaft and head, applying a light flicking touch. If your partner feels relaxed and at ease, her sounds and movements should let you know when you have arrived at an area and a touch that really turns her on. Stay there for a while—long enough to get into the rhythm of the moment but not so long as to desensitize her or cause pain, as can sometimes happen.

One woman described what she likes best, at least at first, as "lapping." "You know, like a dog lapping the bottom of an ice cream carton," she said with an embarrassed laugh. "Rhythmical, insistent, and not missing anything."

Some women like to start with direct stimulation of the clitoris or clitoral shaft—sucking, tonguing, flicking—while others for whom the area is too sensitive for direct touch prefer the stimulation provided indirectly on the surrounding areas.

To increase her arousal, insert one or two fingers in her vagina. Many women say that as they become aroused through clitoral stimulation, even to the point of orgasm, they want to feel something inside them. You can also fondle her breasts and nipples and caress and stroke her entire body while you are devoting your oral attentions to her genitals. One woman reports that during oral sex she and her lover become so excited they actually levitate—or at least she does. "I'm arching my back and pelvis to get more pressure, and he's grabbing me around my ass, and pretty soon I'm up way off the bed, right in his face!"

Anal intercourse

There are three iron-clad rules of anal intercourse: keep it clean, go v-e-r-y slowly, and never force the issue.

For reasons of possible pain (which can be very real) and assocations that some people find unsexy in the extreme, anal intercourse is not for everyone. Those who practice it experience a kind of sensation no other form of intercourse provides. For the man, the tightness of the sphincter muscle ring can provide an exquisite pleasure vaginal intercourse does not offer. For the woman, there are sensations that seem to come from the inside out, instead of the outside in. As one woman wondered, "It feels as if my vagina is being massaged. Is that possible?"

If this is something you and your partner want to

try, make sure you have a lubricant handy for your penis and her anus. Baby oil, vegetable oil, or lubricatory jelly (not vaseline, it's not water solubled) will all work. So will saliva, although not so well. Lying on your sides, spoon fashion, is a good position to start with. It minimizes initial pain, and provides comfort and support while both of you take it one step at a time.

After you are both well lubricated, press your penis against her anal opening. Do not thrust further until you can feel her sphincter muscle relax. She may want you to stimulate her clitoris to ease this process.

If you do so, be sure your hand is clean. *Never* touch her genitals with anything that has penetrated her anal opening without careful washing first. This can and often will cause infection.

After her sphincter muscle has relaxed, you can proceed to enter her further without fear of causing pain. But go slowly and be prepared to stop at any point if she wants to. Communication is important at all phases during anal sex—it can be too overwhelming for the woman if she feels you're not right there with her.

What about Dr. Peter?

I was talking to a friend of mine about women's feelings concerning the à la carte side of the lovemaking menu. What I told him soon had a worried look on his face. "What about old Dr. Peter?" he asked, his coyness hiding some real fear. "Sounds like there isn't much room for him in all these goings-on."

Rest assured. All the manual and oral stimulation in the world will never replace the male member. Here is what some women I talked to had to say on the subject:

"There comes a time when I just want to feel his

penis inside me, to be filled up, to have it pounding in. It's never complete without that."

"I love oral sex. But the thing I don't like about it is that he's way down there, and he feels so far away. After a while, I want him up with me."

"Part of making love for me is being surrounded by someone—feeling their weight, being in their arms, having them inside me."

"I have to admit I usually come to orgasm faster when my lover goes down on me. But intercourse is still the ultimate experience for me. It's the blending, you know, that indescribable feeling of total abandon and total closeness, when no one is doing anything *to* anyone. You're both part of something bigger."

If these reassurances still aren't good enough for you, you might want to take a look at your own attitudes. "These women," you may be thinking. "They haven't met *me*! I'll show them what making love with a penis, the *right* way, is all about! I'll have them begging for it!"

These words represent a good example of hardline, last-ditch sexual illiteracy. Few men these days would actually say them out loud, but a surprising number might think them.

Don't allow yourself to get caught in this dead-end position. Instead of getting defensive, try to broaden your horizons. The man who can honestly see standard genital intercourse as part of a larger repertoire of other sexual techniques is well on his way to becoming an accomplished lover. There are payoffs all around. He's taking a great deal of performance pressure off himself, which will enhance his own enjoyment. And he's also opening the door to an almost infinite variety of lovemaking designed to pleasure himself and his partner.

It's really a no-lose situation.

CHAPTER EIGHT

Intercourse

You have established the mood, let your partner know she is special and cared for, and engaged in exciting and imaginative lovemaking that has given you both great pleasure. You want to create a wonderful experience that will bring the two of you closer together— one that she will always remember, one that will express your virility as well as your tenderness and your vulnerability.

And the demonstration of having achieved these goals will be . . . the quality of her orgasm.

Forget it. If this describes your line of thinking, you have fallen into a complicated trap apparently created for the sexually enlightened man. It goes something like this: if men have been woefully ignorant of women's bodies and needs for all these years and if they finally learn what women want in bed, then doesn't it stand to reason that they should be able to "give" women orgasms—and further, that if they don't, they have failed?

Ironically, making the man responsible for a woman's reaction places a heavy responsibility on women. As a San Francisco psychotherapist put it, "When men were concerned primarily with satisfying themselves during intercourse, it didn't really matter what the woman's reaction was. Now, the pressure is on her. She'd damn well better have an orgasm—and a good one—or her partner has failed, and she has failed twice: once on her own behalf and once on his."

Women echo this sentiment. "It's great when a

man takes the trouble to please me," an attorney in Los Angeles said, "but if it seems that's *all* he's doing, I end up feeling on the spot. I want to know he's pleasing himself too, and then I don't have to worry so much. Does that sound crazy?"

In a sense the greatest gift of lovemaking you can give a woman is to let her know you are enjoying yourself, and in so doing give her permission to do the same. This may at first sound to you like the rankest kind of male chauvinism, but it can lead you *and* your partner into deeper and more intense lovemaking. In the first place, there are few aphrodisiacs more powerful for a woman than seeing her partner literally lose himself in sexual pleasure. "Sometimes, while I'm making love, I'll open my eyes and see my lover's face. He's got his eyes closed, and he's obviously totally carried away with what's happening. It makes me feel so many things to see that—powerfully female, ultimately desirable, and even more turned on."

Furthermore, in the process of letting go yourself you provide your partner the space she may need to do the same. Despite the "merging into one" that characterizes the best lovemaking, there is at the moment of orgasm an almost solitary quality, in which each of you becomes lost in your own feelings, and unaware, at some level, of the other person. One woman described this moment as floating off. "I reach the point where I'm not aware of him, only of my body and the waves of sensations that are going through it. They just carry me away."

What Can You Do To Help?

Perhaps the first thing you can do to help her reach an orgasm is not to push her into one, if it's not her intent. There are many times when a woman is interested in making love but not necessarily in having an orgasm. This occasional preference is at such odds with the masculine experience that many men have a hard time accepting it as valid. Instead they turn it into a comment either on their own inadequacies ("I guess she doesn't think I can give her an orgasm, so she just isn't bothering") or their partners' sexual problems.

Women who don't trust their own feelings can buy into the same thinking. "I used to think there was something wrong with me because I didn't have an orgasm every time," one woman said. "My boyfriend thought there was something wrong with *him*. It took a long time with each other for us to get comfortable with the fact that I just didn't *want* one every time we made love."

Is this something you can ask her directly? Yes, although probably not unless you and she are really comfortable with each other. Sometimes you can create an opening in which she can volunteer the information. "You seem really relaxed and floating," you might say. "I'm afraid I might leave you behind." If there is no hidden accusation in your voice, she may feel free to tell you to go ahead. Then you can both enjoy the experience in the way that fits each of you.

At other times, your partner may indeed want to reach an orgasm. You may sense it from some tenseness in her body, or a certain kind of inward concentration on her part. If you think you are doing all the right things and it's still not happening for her, here are some approaches you might want to consider.

First of all, it is possible that she needs to become more comfortable and knowledgeable about her own body—what it looks like, how it feels, where the erogenous zones are, how she likes to become aroused, and how she likes to reach orgasm. This may call for some private self-exploration on her own, separate from you. If this is the case, you should not take it personally. Just keep in mind that eventually the results of her self-knowledge will benefit both of you.

However, there are some steps you can take with her to help her take off.

Massage

You might want to try a no-intercourse massage with her. It can be sensual, but make sure she understands she will be under no pressure to perform. You don't have to be an expert in massage techniques. Nor should you concentrate only on giving *her* pleasure. Do what turns you on as well. Focusing on your own enjoyment as well as hers will reduce the pressure she may be feeling to "do the right things"—or, even more anxiety-provoking, "*feel* the right things."

Slow down

It may seem to you that you are taking twice as much time in your preliminary lovemaking as you ever did before. You might be right—and from her point of view, you still could be rushing things.

Try building in some plateaus to your lovemaking. Many men—and women too, for that matter—think that lovemaking should be a slow-building, steady climb in which both partners gradually reach a crescendo (preferably at the same time) and then subside. If in this process they reach a plateau during which the sexual intensity levels out or subsides, they panic and do everything they can to flog it back to a fever pitch again.

Accomplished lovers appreciate these plateaus as momentary pauses, pleasurable in and of themselves, that permit them to scale even greater heights. "During an evening of lovemaking I always gain and lose an erection several times before having an orgasm," a Napa Valley carpenter said. "How else could you last for so many hours? But the tension still builds and builds, and when the orgasm finally happens, it's incredible!"

Some couples take a break by switching locations, showering together, or just relaxing and listening to music. "If I know everything doesn't have to happen right away," an artist's model reported, "I can relax and not worry about any pressure. We do some weird things. Once we got some body paints for lovers. We painted each other all over, and then got in this big tub he has, and the paint turned into bubble bath. It was silly, but sexy silly. 'Awaken your senses,' the label said. It was right on."

Communicate

Telling your partner what you like and don't like is difficult for almost all of us—and especially for women, who have been culturally conditioned not to take that kind of responsibility in sexual matters.

There is more to communicating than making direct statements or asking direct questions. Through observation and sensitivity, you can often become aware of what pleases your partner without having to ask.

However, not even the most sensitive lovers are mind readers. Moments arise when a few well-chosen words can make all the difference between frustration and ecstasy. You can set the stage by sharing your own reactions—"Oh, yes! Keep it up, but slower, slower . . ."—and also by gently asking a few questions: "More?" "Is that the right place?" Keep in mind you're not asking for reassurance or compliments, just information.

As in other delicate situations, humor can be the least threatening approach. I know a couple who both wear glasses and are therefore familiar with the trial-and-error method eye doctors employ to prescribe corrective lenses. "Which way is better?" the man will ask, while they are making love. "That way . . . or this way?"

Humor is tricky, though. When it comes to making love, most of us are so vulnerable that even the best-intentioned humorous remark can become cutting. You may think you are using humor to handle your self-consciousness; she may hear it as a criticism about her.

Also, while humor can be a marvelous way to get through an embarrassing situation, even the gentlest humor can be distancing. This is the last thing you want to happen while you are making love. One woman complained that every time she and her lover went to bed, he'd say, "Okay, it's time to make the big red lights go on."

"It didn't totally spoil the mood," she said, "but it did make the whole experience sound a little mechanical."

Also, too much snappy patter of any kind can kill passion. One couple I talked to were highly verbal copywriters for San Francisco ad agencies, but when it came to making love, words failed them—the right words, that is. "We finally just had to agree to shut up," Frank said, "because we didn't seem able to say the right things to each other. It was good for us to learn to communicate without all the verbiage. We became more aware of our feelings and less aware of our brains."

One of the biggest hurdles to overcome in communicating about sex is facing the fact that you have to communicate at all. You may have read that "enlightened" lovers have no trouble letting their partners know just exactly what they like and don't like. The truth is that we all live with the fantasy that if our partners *really* loved us, words would not be necessary.

Wrong. Words are necessary. So keep your communications direct, use "show and tell" whenever possible, and stay as current as possible. If you postpone talking about something you don't like, you run the risk of building a wall of misunderstanding between you and your partner.

By the same token, don't save all your communication for things you don't like or for times when problems arise. One man I talked to said he avoided this trap by exchanging information very early on. "I run my hands over her body," he told me, "and I tell her what I like to do with every part. When I get to her breasts, for example, I say, 'I love it when you roll your breasts back and forth, across my lips, like this.' And I encourage her to tell me what she likes to do and to have me do too. Then we each know what the other likes *before* we do it wrong. I also find it very erotic to say the words."

For many people, in fact, talking about making love during the act itself is a powerful stimulant. It doesn't have to be "dirty talk," although that turns some people on. Simply verbalizing what you are doing—or want to do—can be extremely exciting. "I love hearing myself say the words," a secretary confessed. "It makes the whole experience more real, somehow, and more exciting."

Positions for intercourse

The Frenchman was boasting of his nation's sexual sophistication to an American friend. "In my country," he bragged, "we have one hundred positions for making love."

"One hundred!" exclaimed the American, wide-eyed. "Well, let's see, there's the man lying on top of the woman . . ."

"*Mon Dieu!*" the Frenchman interrupted. "One hundred and one!"

Many people seeking to expand their sexual horizons think the answer lies in experimenting with various lovemaking positions. The truth is that most couples—and most individuals—sooner or later discover one or two positions that give them the most pleasure and they stick with these. Still, variety can indeed spice up your lovemaking, especially if you understand the physical and psychological advantages and disadvantages to each position.

What makes certain positions more enjoyable to some people than others? The answers lie in the particular physical fit between two people, the psychological support offered in various positions, and the types of stimulation each position encourages and inhibits.

Research also suggests a link between how women masturbate and the position for intercourse they find most stimulating. If they masturbate lying passively while fondling their genitals, they may be brought to orgasm most quickly by a position in which their partner is able to do the same to them. If they stimulate their clitorises directly during masturbation, they will respond best to a position for intercourse that provides direct clitoral stimulation.

The missionary position

Surveys indicate that women differentiate between those positions that give the greatest psychological satisfaction and those that offer the greatest opportunity for physical release.

In the former category, the man-on-top, or "missionary" position wins hands down. Sixty-one percent of the respondents in *The Cosmo Report* preferred this position. They reported that they felt more "protected" and "enveloped" and less exposed and vulnerable than if they were on top.

This finding is matched by a similar male preference. To most men in Western society, being on top seems "more natural," more supportive of the image they want of themselves as males who are dominant and in control. In addition, many men find they achieve the best physical stimulation in this position because they can control the depth and timing of their thrusts.

What women like is the front-to-front, top-to-bottom contact of the missionary position. "I like feeling absolutely glued to him," one woman said. "I can see him, feel him, be with him totally when he's on top of me."

Nevertheless, they do not necessarily find this position best for reaching orgasm. "To some extent I can control things by raising my legs," one woman reported. "But I can't always get the kind of clitoral stimulation I need. Also, there's just no way to establish the right rhythm. It's almost completely up to my lover; sometimes it just doesn't work out."

The woman on top

In years past, the idea of the woman assuming the "dominant" position during sex went against all our cultural conditioning. Being on the bottom was unmanly, inappropriate; being on top was unfeminine, inappropriate. However, for purposes of reaching orgasm, most women prefer this position, and more and more are not hesitating to say so.

"I can establish just the speed and rhythm I want," says one woman. "I can easily position myself to stimulate my clitoris, instead of having to struggle to do it when he's on top of me," says another. "It's less overwhelming, somehow. I feel more in control of what's happening," says a third.

If you can get over the standard male hang-up about being on the bottom, various sexual pleasures await you. In the first place, it is an ideal position from which to appreciate, fondle and kiss her breasts. Secondly, if you know she's in charge of the pacing, you can stop worrying about whether you're "doing it right" for her. Many women report that they can prolong intercourse in this position by slowing down at times their partners wouldn't be able to. "I watch him," one woman said, "and when I see he's getting close, I just stop for a minute. We can go on for much longer this way."

Finally, the feeling of being "done to" can be exquisitely and surprisingly pleasurable, especially if you are the kind of man who always thinks he has to be in charge and on top of things. "The first time my girlfriend and I made love this way, I thought I would feel sort of dumb," a computer consultant said. "But it was an easy turn-on, just lying there.

She bent over and slowly swung her breasts back and forth across my chest and lips, tantalizing me. She just kept me going for hours, it seemed."

From the rear

Jeff had had a fantasy for some time about entering his girlfriend's vagina from the rear, but had never had the nerve to bring it up. "I thought she would feel degraded or something," he said. "But one night it just finally happened. She loved it! I loved it!"

Rear-entry positions include lying on your side behind your partner, like two spoons; lying stretched out on top of your partner—or with your partner on her hands and knees before you. "When we do it doggy-style, I get this very sexy, wanton feeling of being totally exposed and at his mercy," a secretary reported. "It's also the best position for stimulating my clitoris, either by my lover or by me. And the sight of my ass wriggling around is a real turn-on, my lover says."

Side by side

Lying on your sides facing each other is friendly, relaxed, flexible, and perfectly suitable for falling asleep in each other's arms without having to move. It can also be comfortable if one of you is a lot taller than the other.

Getting into it in the first place can take a little bit of arranging. One way is to start in the missionary position with your penis already inserted. Then, as she draws up her right leg, you both roll over (to your left) until you are lying on your sides facing each other. For a better fit, you may want to grasp her lower leg between your thighs. (There is an additional advantage to this position if one of you is left-handed, in that you can arrange to lie on the side that will give that person the greatest use of the left hand.)

In this position you don't have to worry about supporting your weight on your elbows and knees, and she doesn't have to worry about feeling suffocated. Many couples find this position encourages a kind of cozy intimacy that suits them perfectly.

Variations

Beyond the basics, there are some variations that you can employ to add a fillip to your lovemaking, if you're so inclined.

Sitting up, with your partner's legs wrapped around your waist, can make you think you are part of an ancient Persian miniature, X-rated version. Opportunities for deep thrusting are somewhat limited, but it's an excellent position if you want to postpone orgasm as long as possible. "I like it once in a while," said a woman of wide experience. "If the man has some other tricks in his bag besides simple screwing, it allows him to show them off. Also, even though you're together you can lean back and take in the other person visually."

Try having your partner lean/lie back at the edge of the bed, or the bureau, or the laundry table—or whatever other object is the right height for both of you. You remain standing, and enter her from that position. Many women like this variation because the tilt of their pelvis allows the man access to their clitoris with his fingers. (In fact, women tend to like any position that allows manual stimulation of their clitorises during intercourse itself—either by the man or by themselves.)

Bending her over a piece of furniture is another position worth experimenting with. It enables you to thrust deeply and at your own rhythm, and for some women it offers psychological as well physical stimulation. Reports one woman from Portland: "My boyfriend and I have this little routine where I play his secretary and he's the boss, and we do it with me leaning over the desk. Yes, the desk is hard, but it's fun every so often."

That's the thing about variations. It's often their differentness that makes them enjoyable, rather than anything about the position itself—although you never know until you try. One woman said she and her lover sometimes make love standing up: "The first time we did it he showed me how to raise up my leg by putting it in the loop of a belt that he had hitched over the bedroom doorknob. He said prostitutes in Europe do that in back alleys for quickies on a cold night. Or you can pull out a bureau drawer to get just the right height for you."

When's the best time to try out variations? Whenever the spirit moves. Many people find it easier to start out with something a little more exotic for initial stimulation and then switch over to a tried-and-true position when they get down to business.

On the other hand, if you anticipate making love for a long time, there's something to be said for switching positions at some point midway during the evening (or morning, or afternoon), to give you both time to pause and regroup. Another advantage is that a new position permits stimulation of slightly different areas of your genitals and hers. Sometimes simply switching the sensory focus will significantly enhance your mutual pleasure.

Finally, there's something about simply taking the trouble to be inventive that many women appreciate. "One of the things I like about my lover is that he's always dreaming up new ways to make love," a willowy brunette real estate agent reported. "Sometimes they're a little strange, but I love it that he thinks about it. I can just imagine him at work, silently figuring out something new and whacky to surprise me with."

If she's a virgin

To stress the physical aspects of making love to a virgin is to miss the point almost completely. Her hymen *may* be still intact—although it may have already been stretched or broken through vigorous exercise or gynecological examinations. *If* it is intact, it *may* bleed upon being broken. There *may* be considerable pain and bleeding. It is possible that if the hymen is thick and tough enough, a surgical procedure may be necessary to remove it.

The man's responsibility, physically speaking, is clear enough: go slowly, don't force anything, and if intolerable pain ensues, stop completely.

It's the emotional impact you want to be thinking about. Of all the "first times" in a person's life, male or female, this "first time" has got to rank among the very most important. If your partner tells you she's a virgin, yours is the responsibility for initiating her into the pleasures of making love. The experience she shares with you may color her subsequent attitudes more than any other single sexual experience. (Of course, if you are also a virgin, you will probably need a little tenderness and understanding yourself.)

Keep in mind that what she needs from you most is patience, caring, reassurance—and more reassurance. Take every cue from her. This is perhaps the one time when you can focus all your attention on orchestrating a moment only for her and give your own needs and desires second priority.

And don't take it personally if she doesn't have an orgasm. Many women do not the first time they make love—or even the first time they make love with a particular partner. As one woman remembered, "The first time I made love, I was so overwhelmed with the significance of the act that I couldn't really get much from the act itself. It was lovely, though, because the man and I—he was just a boy, really—

cared a lot for each other, and he was very, very gentle."

Having said all this, I must report that a few of the women I discussed virginity with gave the horse laugh to what one called the "macho virgin trip." "Spare me this 'be gentle with me' stuff," she said. "I hate to spoil your strong-protector fantasies, but it isn't always a big deal with women. When I was eighteen, I decided it was high time I did it, so I did it. Nice, but no big deal. I did take a good long look at myself in the mirror afterward, though, to see if I looked any different. I bet all women do that. Men too, maybe?"

CHAPTER NINE

The Big O and the Little G

While endless potency is something all males dream about at various times in their lives, it's a fantasy that has more to do with conquest and power than with making love, or even enjoying sex.

The late Ali Khan, international playboy, husband to Rita Hayworth and the reputed lover of untold numbers of lovely and willing women throughout the world, was said to have mastered an ancient Eastern sexual technique that enabled him to make love literally for hours at a stretch without either reaching orgasm or losing his erection. The secret of this technique is primarily mental; to oversimplify things considerably, it involves "thinking about something else."

The fact of the matter is, however, it is women, not men, who have been naturally graced with multiple and various orgasmic powers. Yet despite serious and well-funded research in recent years, the nature and physiology of the female orgasm remains something of a mystery. Is there one type, or are there two or more? Is there a single and specific pleasure point, or several? Is it the clitoris? The G spot? Some other still-undiscovered place?

While these questions occupy sex researchers throughout the world, they seem of less concern to women themselves. Without question, advances in knowledge about the sexual physiology of the female have helped many women learn how to enhance their sexuality. Yet at least among the women I talked to, the "seat of orgasm" issue was not a burning one. As one exasperated children's book editor said, "What's with this G spot? I can't even *find* my G spot. I have enough trouble finding a *date!*"

"For me an orgasm happens or it doesn't happen," a user-friendly computer programmer reported. "I see patterns, but I can't isolate the variables. It's just a total experience. Frankly, this search for women's 'hot spots' make me a little impatient."

Impatience is not the feeling engendered in some men by this quest. With each heavy-breathing announcement of yet another breakthrough in women's orgasmic potential, many males are likely to sink further into panic and confusion. Lamented a male free-lance writer, "It's like constantly getting upgraded software for my word processor. I just begin to figure out the new functions, and they come up with different ones to learn."

What makes women have orgasms?

Researchers have identified the physiological changes that women go through when they become aroused toward orgasm. The nipples engorge with blood, swell, and become stiff. The flow of blood to the pelvic and genital area also increases. The vagina starts to secrete lubricants; the vaginal lips, inner and outer, enlarge, as does the clitoris.

As orgasm nears, the pulse rate increases, the upper body reddens, and the feet and hands tense up. Sometimes the muscles in the face start to contract. At this point the vagina will also begin contractions.

Orgasm itself, much like the man's experience, occurs when all this tension—of muscles and blood pressure—reaches a maximum point and is then released. Vaginal contractions increase in frequency, along with contractions of the uterus. With the relaxation of the muscles and the circulation of the blood back to other parts of the body comes the feeling of warmth and peace and "doneness" that lets the woman know she has reached a climax and achieved sexual release.

This, clinically stated, is the physiological response. What makes it happen?

Ask any woman what kind of lovemaking results in an orgasm for her, and she is likely to list such conditions as feeling close to the man, feeling sexy, feeling loved and appreciated, feeling relaxed, and not feeling anxious.

Are hot buttons important? Well, yes and no. On the one hand, women downplay the mechanical aspects of making love, especially when talking to a man—partly because they don't want to play into the traditional male's mechanical "insert part A into part B" approach and partly because the former conditions simply must be present before button pushing has any effect.

"There are some evenings," one woman said, "when I'm out with a man and I know we're going to make love and I know I'm ripe for an orgasm. Maybe it's the way he looks at me at dinner, or makes physical contact with me . . . just anything to let me know he finds me attractive. Then, we sort of get a rhythm going between us, and we start focusing more and more on each other. I just loosen up and start to feel sexy."

The answer to the question "What makes women have orgasms?" then, comes in two parts. First and foremost, the feelings must be right. Only then do the more clinical aspects of erotic stimulation come into play. Too many men bring a reversed emphasis to their lovemaking and then wonder why they have to work so hard to make their partners' fireworks explode. This approach is a guaranteed turnoff to women. As one told me, "I can always tell when a guy thinks he's going to 'play me like a violin.' It's a performance on his part to demonstrate how good he is, and I just hate it. It makes me feel so . . . distant from him."

How to arouse women nonphysically during intercourse

It never occurs to most men to stress the purely emotional during the act of love itself. This is the time, they assume, when they can and should finally get totally physical. Even the most sophisticated lover, totally wrapped up in giving his partner exquisite physical sensations, may not always realize the power that the nonphysical expression of his feelings will have on her.

"I knew a man who kept his eyes open all the time we made love," a bubbly travel agent with ash-blond hair told me. "I felt like I was looking directly into his soul, right up to—and into—orgasm. That may be the definition of absolute, total, and complete contact with another person."

Feelings are funny things. Most of us go to great lengths to hide them, even the ones we want others to know about, usually because we fear being exposed and vulnerable. What if they're not reciprocated? What if we look foolish? What if we can't handle the response we get?

But feelings, honestly expressed, are the best way to touch another person. In fact, they are really the only way. To a great extent, of course, you express your feelings physically when you make love, but if you ignore the nonphysical altogether, you are missing a good bet.

When Pam and her boyfriend were settling in to their relationship, they each went to great lengths to please the other in bed. Both wanted the relationship to continue and grow; each wanted the sex to be good and so they tried hard—so hard, in fact, that the effort began to get in their way.

"One time David was contorted in some weird position trying to do eight things at once," she remembers, "and I caught a glimpse of the expression on his face. It was pure exasperation. My heart just went out to him. He saw me watching him, and . . . well, it was a moment of real contact for both of us, one that we didn't have to try for."

To turn a woman on with your feelings, you first have to know what they are—and be prepared for the fact that they may not always be loving passion. Making love can sometimes uncover powerful emotions of anger. In the right circumstances, expressing them can be both cleansing and tremendously stimulating.

Howard and his wife, Elena, were tax accountants who shared a practice. In order to spend twenty-four hours a day in each other's company, much of that time as professional colleagues, they had unconsciously adopted a certain distance and formality with each other. "Polite," Howard says. "God, we were polite. Nothing ever got dealt with between us. We just didn't feel we could risk a big blowout."

Then came one night when they were making love. "We had been making love less and less," Howard remembers. "But anyway, that night there we were, down to the short strokes, as they say, and I suddenly realized I was really pissed off at this woman. I mean really pissed off! So all of a sudden it became a matter of 'Take that, you bitch! And that! And that!'

"I looked down at her and I could see she was really angry too. Her face was just contorted in anger. We were screwing each other in every sense of the word. Well, we just took off and went with it, and it was fantastic! The best sex I can remember! And as you can probably guess, we weren't angry afterward."

Adds Elena, "I think it was such a turn-on for me because I finally felt him there physically *and* emotionally—with me, in me, connected to me. The energy within himself that he let out that night was tremendously erotic and liberating for me. I responded totally."

You should know, however, that unleashing your anger does not automatically clear the air, or enhance closeness. For that to happen, there must be love—and trust—between the two of you. Assured of these, you and your partner can then hear—and even get turned on by—each other's anger and other strong feelings.

So if some of your censored feelings have been casting a pall on your relationship, you might experiment with letting them out in the arena of making love. But before—and after—you do, make sure she knows that you love and cherish her and do not intend to allow this temporary stormy weather to cause any permanent damage.

Types of orgasm

Despite the fact that they stress the nonmechanical aspects, women do not usually achieve orgasms spontaneously. Here we run up against one of women's most-repeated grievances about men: their ignorance of a woman's sexual anatomy. "I don't get it," one woman told me. "Men apparently spend every waking minute focused on how to get into a woman's pants, but they don't seem to know the first thing about what to do once they get there."

Fran, fiftyish, is the dean of students at a northern California women's college. She was a virgin until the age of twenty-three, when her first sexual experience resulted in an orgasmic experience that, quite literally, left her quaking. "I just couldn't stop coming," she remembers. "For twenty-four hours I walked around having vaginal contractions. It was incredible. I really must have been ready for sex."

Ask seven different women to describe an orgasm and you are likely to get seven different answers— partly, they will tell you, because different orgasms feel different, but also, obviously, because it's not something you can measure against a commonly accepted standard.

"A warmth, a tingling sensation in my genitals,"

"slow waves of feeling that carry me with them," "a sharp, brief spasm sort of like a sneeze," "I start by feeling suspended, floating and tingling and getting warmer and warmer"—these are the words some women have used to say what an orgasm feels like. Other women describe much more powerful experiences. "It's a something that starts deep inside me and radiates out and out and out," one woman reported. Said another, "Like the surf crashing over both of us."

Many women think they have been having orgasms until they find a sexual partner with whom they reach previously unexplored heights. "With Jerry sex was good," said a young woman from Las Vegas, "but more like a soft, warm glow that didn't really have a focus. With Tom, the earth moves. Tom seems to know more about a woman's body. He's so caring and patient."

Early research into female orgasm went round and round, trying to isolate various types and placing psychological and even political value judgments on which were "best" and "most mature." These days, however, the emphasis is less on types of orgasms—an orgasm is generally held to be an orgasm—than on its source or sources.

What the researchers have found—and what most women concur with—is that the clitoris, directly or indirectly, is what makes it happen. Without the kind of clitoral stimulation she likes, a woman is not likely to have an orgasm. In some cases she can get this kind of stimulation during intercourse.

"If I can get in a position to rub my clitoral area against him just right, I can reach an orgasm during intercourse," a woman reported. "Or if he enters from the rear, I can rub against the bed."

For most women, however, manual or oral stimulation of the clitoris is a must—and this usually means foreplay. "You know the song about the lover with a s-l-o-w hand?" one woman asked. "That's what I want, somebody who can be gentle and slow and take his time."

Some women say that having an orgasm through manual or oral stimulation before intercourse guarantees that they can climax again during intercourse itself. Others prefer to wait. "I've got my lover trained," a student claimed. "He goes down on me until I get so hot I can't stand it. When I tell him to stop, he enters me, and I have an orgasm almost immediately."

The Grafenberg spot

If the clitoris is ultimately what makes it happen, there is also evidence to suggest that there may be more involved.

Many researchers describe two kinds of orgasms. Although they use different words, the difference seems to be between generalized, sharply focused sensation almost like a spasm, and a deeper, more generalized reaction that spreads through a woman's body and goes on pulsating for a much longer period of time. This second type can contain peaks and plateaus—"a heightened sexual state," as one woman described it, "that goes far beyond just 'getting off.' "

This second kind of orgasm—the earth mover—almost always involves vaginal penetration, usually following more specific attentions to the clitoris. "When my lover enters from the rear," one woman said, "he can play with my clitoris at the same time. When he does that, the feeling of his penis inside me adds an entirely new dimension."

This is the "deeper" orgasm involving more of the body than the genitals alone. Its triggering point may be what is now known as the Grafenberg spot, or G spot, named after Ernst Grafenberg, the German physician who described it for the first time in 1950.

The G spot is located about two inches inside the

vagina, on the surface toward the navel, just behind the pubic bone. About the size of a dime or small bean, it consists of blood vessels, glands and ducts, and nerve endings. These are pelvic nerves, different from those serving the clitoral area.

When the G spot is stimulated, it becomes firmer and more defined to the touch. Upon orgasm, the uterus and deep pelvic muscles begin their contractions—slower and longer-lasting than those triggered by clitoral stimulation. The result is the kind of total orgasm that one woman described as being to a clitoral orgasm "what a 747 is to a Piper Cub."

Helping her reach deep orgasm

You can learn to read your partner's progress toward orgasm by sensing differences in the movements within her vagina.

During initial clitoral stimulation, the vagina expands and becomes wider and deeper. This will feel to your inserted fingers like a loosening. Simultaneously, you may feel some rhythmic clenching of the vaginal walls. At this point your partner may want you to continue stimulating her clitoris, although its heightened sensitivity may dictate lighter, more teasing strokes.

Now begin to stimulate her G spot, experimenting with rhythm and pressure until you find a combination she likes. Keep up this stroking for ten to twelve even cycles. Lighten up, then resume stroking.

Eventually—depending on you, the woman, and the moment, it can take five minutes, thirty, or longer—you will feel a different kind of contraction, as if the vagina were closing up and pushing out. This is the result of contractions of the uterus and deep pelvic muscles, which signal the beginning of the deep orgasm.

To continue to heighten her pleasure, you can back off from the G spot and return to her clitoris.

Eventually, you will discover an alternating pattern of stimulations and pauses between the clitoris and the G spot that will produce both the vaginal and the uterine contractions. Women who have experienced these describe the combination as the ultimate. As one puts it, "This is when time stops. You just stop trying; everything happens all by itself."

According to the researchers, it takes conscious effort to be able to achieve this kind of orgasmic experience. The effort can eventually pay off, they claim, in a permanently heightened sexual state that eventually makes orgasms possible almost immediately after penetration. Like Fran, who was orgasmic for twenty-four hours, a woman in this state may go through the day after making love at or just below the threshold of vaginal contractions.

This might explain the remark of one woman I talked to. "When I'm between lovers or not very sexually active," she said, "I can go for a long time without needing to make love. I don't avoid it; I just don't think about it. But if I'm involved with a man, and the sex is good, I really get horny. The better it is, the more I think about it. All I want to do is get into bed with him."

Faking it

Can you tell when a woman fakes an orgasm? Absolutely—if you're making love in a laboratory and have all her appropriate body parts wired up to the right machinery. Otherwise, it will probably depend on how well you know her and just how sensitive you are to her responses in general. Many men claim to have discovered various signs of undeniable excitement—a certain moan, a telltale flush, a specific change in breathing—but since each woman reacts differently, these indications are valid only when you and your partner have a long history together.

A better question to ask yourself is, why do you want to know? If you are motivated by wanting to increase her sexual pleasure, the best way to find out is to ask her. Not, obviously, right after making love—and probably not phrased in that way. What you need to do is back up and talk about the kinds of lovemaking she likes so that she won't feel the need to fake anything.

Women fake orgasms because they feel pressure to do so. In these days when everyone is supposed to be totally orgasmic, the pressure can be internal. It's also true that a woman will sometimes fake a climax just to get sex over with. More often, however, when a woman fakes an orgasm it's because she thinks her man expects her to have one, and she doesn't want to disappoint him.

"It's just another way women take care of men," one woman told me. "You've got to let them know they have been so devastatingly good in bed that you were carried off to the heights. You somehow end up feeling guilty."

To avoid the distance and resentment this attitude engenders, shift your focus away from orgasm as the be-and-end-all of making love, concentrate more on the pleasure of lovemaking itself—and, most important, communicate this emphasis to your partner. You don't need to make a speech to get this point across. Let her know by sharing with her the pleasure you get from every moment of making love with her.

As one man said, "If you think about it, when a man has an orgasm, it's all over anyway, at least for a while. Why not think about extending what comes before? That's where the fun is."

A final word on "technique"

A puzzling irony for many men is the fact that in one breath women will talk about the specific things

they want men to do while making love to them—
and in the next will claim that they don't like making love with a man who seems "too accomplished."

"What do they think," one man exclaimed to me in
exasperation, "that it's all supposed to come naturally?
Well, what if it doesn't?"

Women's objections to the accomplished lover are
really aimed at how they perceive these accomplish-
ments being used. What they *don't* like are men who
display their sexual prowess as just that—a display
of expertise rather than a means of bringing pleasure.
"I don't know what it is," one woman reported, "but
I can be with a man who is doing all the right things,
and instead of getting turned on, my reaction is to
think I should be applauding. I feel like an audience
he is trying to dazzle."

So do learn the techniques, but don't forget that
the reason for learning them in the first place is to
create with your partner a physical *and* emotional
experience that will bring the two of you closer
together. When one of you "performs," the result can
only be distance. And that always leads to trouble.

Most important, remember that creating this experience does not begin with sexual gymnastics, no
matter how accomplished. First, you need to create
an atmosphere in which she feels cherished, cared
for, appreciated, special. In this context your lovemaking skills become an expression of your feelings
toward her and not a demonstration of your profi-
ciency as a lover. It's a distinction that makes all the
difference.

CHAPTER TEN

Afterward

More than foreplay, more than intercourse, more even than orgasm—when it comes to the ingredients that make up a pleasurable sexual experience, it's what comes *afterward* that counts the most. This was the conclusion reached by two psychologists who surveyed *après*-sex behavior in more than 250 cases, and published their findings in a book called *Afterplay: A Key to Intimacy*.

Moreover, they found, couples who can sustain intimacy after making love—instead of drifting off to sleep or into those "I've got to get some gas for the car tomorrow" thoughts—are much more likely to find significant emotional rewards in the experience of making love and in their relationships.

Performance versus relationship questions

That these findings apply most strongly to women is not surprising. What is surprising is that they apply almost as strongly to men.

After you make love, you may be lost in a rosy glow. Or—especially if the relationship is a new one—you may be beset by some nagging questions. Many of them probably boil down to, "Was I good enough?" This typical masculine response follows directly from seeing lovemaking as a performance to be measured. After the performance is over, many men immediately start replaying it in their minds—less to savor the pleasure than to assess how well they did.

Women, on the other hand, are usually on a totally different emotional plane. In the first place, many women do not consider "after orgasm" to be synonymous with "after lovemaking." In fact, for some women, what follows intercourse—the cuddling, the holding, the closeness—is the most important part of the experience. "Lots of times I go to bed with someone mostly just to be held," one shy graduate student revealed. "We have sex because that's what the guy wants, but what I really like is the afterward part. Does that mean I'm not evolved?"

Typically, during these moments a woman's thoughts are on your feelings for her, hers for you, and where the relationship stands now. "I should know better," a fortyish tax accountant said, "but for me it's the moment of truth. If he turns away, or seems to be pulling back emotionally, I get very depressed. Everything that just happened between us feels canceled out, somehow."

"My lover and I have a good relationship," another woman reported, "but I still need him to talk to me, hold me, be with me after we've made love, or else I get an empty feeling, just for a minute, that is sort of scary. I wonder, is it just the sex he wants? It's silly, because I know there's more than that, but I still think about it."

A time of maximum fragility

To make the most of these tender moments after lovemaking, you need to understand that this is indeed some kind of moment of emotional truth. The physical needs that brought you both together have been satisfied and now the emotional underpinnings of your relationship are laid bare.

This is a period of maximum fragility—for you as well as for her. You have both revealed yourselves at your most vulnerable. You have scaled the heights, perhaps lost yourselves totally in out-of-space-and-time passion, and now you are spent and back in the real world.

In some cases, this is the time when it becomes glaringly evident that the only connection between you and your partner is sexual. Kathy, an attractive and capable young nurse who seems to have her fair share of affairs of the heart, remembers a period in her life when she went to great lengths to avoid this part of lovemaking altogether.

"Oh, God!" she remembers. "In those days I was involved with lots of guys who were all wrong for me, and in some part of me I knew it. I could avoid the issue while we were having sex, but afterward—sometimes the truth just hung in the air. I was so nervous about what would happen and how I would feel that I used to find very inventive ways to prolong intercourse."

This is the point at which people in Kathy's position often get up and go home, or wish they could. "You're lying there trying to figure out a graceful way of leaving," a man admitted to me. "Then, when she jumps at whatever lame excuse you come up with, you realize she has been lying there wishing you would go home too."

On the other hand, it's easy to misinterpret your feelings at this point. Almost everyone feels a "little sadness" in these moments. Physiologically, there are good reasons for postcoital feelings of letdown. Your heart and other body systems have had a workout and are now subsiding to normal levels. Also, after you have achieved maximum physical closeness, whatever happens next almost has to feel like separation.

If after making love you feel closer than ever to your partner, that's great. If you don't, don't automatically assume there must be something wrong with the relationship. If you avoid jumping to conclusions, you can create in these moments a warm glow of peace and well-being that can banish your anxiety and sense of isolation.

Said one man on this subject, "In the early stages of a relationship, sometimes I get a little weird right after making love—skittish, maybe, or nervous. It helps if I can maintain contact with my partner—by touching or talking or looking—until these feelings pass."

Some do's and don't's

What women want and need most at this time are closeness and reassurance. So give them, and freely. This is not something anyone likes to *ask* for. "I know you're not supposed to assume people are mind readers," one woman sighed, "but I hate to ask to be held. It makes me feel like I'm imposing, or feeble or something."

Cuddle

The snuggly, cozy connotations of cuddling are all wrong for steamy sex, but all right for its warm afterglow. With passion spent, there is nothing better than lying wrapped in each other's arms—treasuring the shared intimacy, reveling in the sense of having created your private island of security against the outside world. Cutting off these special moments by turning over and going to sleep robs you both of time to enjoy each other's physical closeness with no pressure to *do* anything.

Share

The feelings you share in these moments can give meaning and direction to the physical intimacy you have just experienced. "After I make love," said one woman, "and we're just lying there, I want to know what he's thinking, but sometimes I'm afraid to ask for fear I'll break the mood."

In this context, even the smallest of small talk takes on new meanings of closeness. It is not the best time to get into details of what has just happened, not even to pay compliments. "How was it for you?" or even "That was fantastic!" tends to focus on performance—and may bring to mind comparisons with other people. A better approach is to talk about how you are feeling right now—"I'd like to drift off to sleep in your arms like this every night."

Nibble

Making love can give people healthy appetites. One New York translator has a ritual postcoital meal she likes to indulge in. "Spaghetti," she admitted, "with butter and parmesan cheese. Even though I have to get out of bed to make it, it's what I crave."

A man I know arranges to satisfy munchie needs without breaking the mood by having a plate of fruit and cheese within easy reach of the bed. "It's fun to sit up in bed and have a bite," he says, "and it's sexy to feed each other grapes. Also, if you go to sleep and later want to make love again, eating a piece of fruit can help freshen your mouth."

Bathe . . . together

Nothing puts a wetter blanket on the glow of togetherness than rushing to clean up afterward. If your fastidiousness absolutely requires you to repair to the bathroom for shower or a bath, why not suggest you do it together?

Allow some time

Making love at the end of the evening may be romantic, but it can leave busy people too exhausted to do much more than fall asleep as soon as they are finished. One couple I know reverses the normal order of things. "When we make love early in the evening," he says, "we feel less rushed, and more like extending the experience. We may get up to go out to dinner—or stay in bed and nosh, maybe watch TV, and make love some more. It's totally relaxing."

Try making love in the morning. Many men experience a greater desire for sex when they first wake up in the morning than they do at the end of the day. Staying in bed on a weekend with nothing else to do but make love, doze off, eat something, read the papers, make love again can be the experience that moves a relationship from casual to committed. "Saturday night is serious, heavy-duty stuff," a San Francisco secretary said. "You've got to be on your best behavior. But Sunday morning, things are more normal, hopefully. The papers are all over the bed, and you can relax, be yourself, mess around a little. Sex for me is always better then."

Sex in the morning has its rewards even on Mondays. As one beautician said, "I love passion before breakfast. It gives me a real charge. I've got my little secret to feel good about all day, no matter what terrible things happen."

What if something goes wrong?

Let's face it: sooner or later, a lovemaking experience won't turn out the way you had hoped. You don't get an erection, or you do but it fails you at the critical moment, or any number of other disasters come between you and a satisfactory conclusion. You struggle to salvage something out of the experience (i.e., bring *somebody* to orgasm), but it's not in the cards.

Disappointment and frustration hang so heavy over the bed that they cannot be ignored. What should you do now?

First of all, don't berate yourself. That will only

make you feel worse than you already do. Besides, your partner will then be obligated to come up with a polite reply to each self-abusive remark you make.

Don't overexplain, either. It's one thing to say something like, "I guess I had too much wine," or "That'll teach me to work so many twelve-hour days." It's another to lay out an elaborate defense that blows the experience out of all proportion.

Far more productive is the attitude of a man I talked to about this situation. "I just figure it's going to happen every once in a while, sort of like Russian roulette," he said. "I try not to spend too much time figuring out why. Of course, if it's early in a relationship, it's more embarrassing, but what the hell? There's always the next time."

Nevertheless, you can't always simply ignore what happened. If you and your partner can avoid getting defensive and assigning blame, you can use your feelings to get closer to each other. "I'm feeling disappointed," you might say, holding her in your arms. "How about you?"

If she agrees, and you can hear her agreement without taking it personally (well, *too* personally), you and she have opened up a chance to deepen the intimacy between you—not as you had hoped to do it, perhaps, but in a way that will set the stage for enhanced lovemaking the next time. You might be surprised to discover that, having achieved a new level of intimacy, the next time will happen almost right away.

CHAPTER ELEVEN

Sex Between the Ears

Here's the true-false quiz on sexual fantasies:
1. We fantasize about things we would like to do in "real life" but are too repressed to act out.
2. In the best of all worlds, we would not need fantasies to enhance sexual stimulation.
3. Fantasies reveal the truth of our innermost selves.

If you said false, false, and false, you chalked up a perfect score, but you're in a minority. Thanks to our fascination for psychological symptom hunting, sexual fantasies have gotten something of a bad name. Many people fear that their fantasies reveal too much about themselves. This is one area in which our fear of hidden psychological truth may have outstripped the so-called sexual revolution.

In the past, people shied away from revealing their sexual fantasies for fear they were immoral. Today, many people are almost as reluctant, but now it is for fear of revealing an immature and "unevolved" sexuality. Lurking in our minds is the fear that if we really had our act together, we wouldn't "need" fantasies to express ourselves sexually.

Nevertheless, many researchers today simply don't believe this is true. In the first place, almost all lovemaking has elements of fantasy—romantic fantasy, happily-ever-after fantasy, two-ships-passing-in-the-night fantasy. Any conscious decision to create a mood—with candlelight, soft music, good wine—is also a decision to create a fantasy.

Of course, when people talk about sexual fantasies, they are usually referring to the "you dress up in

Saran Wrap and I'll pour champagne all over you" variety, and even more often to the fantasy rape-and-bondage scenes in which simulated fear and subjugation and some degree of real physical pain play a part.

This latter variety causes some real problems for all the women today who have absolutely no interest in playing the victim in either their personal or professional lives—and yet for whom some kind of sexual experience involving subjugation and even pain is incredibly stimulating.

"Okay, here it is," a successful word-processor sales rep admitted. "I've got a silk scarf next to my bed, and sometimes I ask my lover to tie my hands to the bedpost while we're making love. I writhe around in ecstasy—for me it's a turn-on you wouldn't believe—but afterward I say, 'My God, what's the matter with me?' This is sick, it's regressive, it's everything I don't believe in about women. But I love it!"

As a nation of armchair psychiatrists, it's tempting for us to probe such fantasies for their "real meaning." Perhaps she is punishing herself for being successful in what she still feels, deep down, is a man's world. Perhaps during childhood and adolescence she made associations between sexual pleasure and punishment. Perhaps she is better able to enjoy sex if she doesn't have to take responsibility for her action.

Perhaps. But in the long run, so what? Which is more real, her fantasies or the facts of the life she leads? More and more mental-health professionals are losing patience with the notion that the only truth is the hidden truth. "Unless someone is denying a lot, I don't find it very useful to spend endless hours reading their psychic tea leaves," a Berkeley family therapist told me. "I deal with what's actually happening in their lives, and encourage them to do the same. Eventually, everything comes out."

Besides, researchers now believe that pleasure and pain may be chemical cousins. The stimulus of some degree of pain may be enough to trigger a chemical in the brain similar to the one produced during sexual arousal. The whole matter, in other words, could be much more biochemical than we now believe.

"Let's pretend"

Assuming that you would like to enhance your lovemaking with some erotic fantasy play, just how should you go about doing it?

An absolute must before you do anything is to be sure you and your partner have developed what some people call a "trust base." This takes time. You both need to be sure not only that you will not hurt each other physically, but that you will accept each other's secret wishes without judging or ridiculing them.

The major hurdle is bringing up the subject in the first place. You can ease into things by making more use of your theatrical sense in all aspects of your relationship. Start by planning some things to do that build in elements of playacting. I know a portrait artist in San Francisco who likes to take women on turn-of-the-century picnics. "It's fun to dress up," he says. "I wear my peasant shirt and beret, and my girlfriend puts on something lacy, and we take wine and cheese and a big loaf of bread in an old basket. No processed foods or canned drinks or anything modern. I have a secret place we go near the redwoods, and after lunch we can get totally naked and make love. I feel like I'm a French Impressionist out with his artist's model."

One woman was delighted when she came home one evening to discover that her lover had transformed the house into a dimly lit grotto—no lights, just candles and more candles everywhere. "He was wearing a pair of very thin cotton drawstring pants, no shirt," she remembers, "and greeted me at the door with a glass of wine. 'I am here to serve you,' he said. He'd fixed a dinner of cold chicken and fruit and we ate it on the floor on some pillows he'd arranged. He'd found some special oil for massage and ... well, I ravished him. It sounds corny now, but it was very sexy at the time."

Sometimes the simple act of making love in a different part of the house can add a new erotic dimension to the experience. "It sounds funny," one woman said, "because I love to make love in bed, but there's something about a hard, cold surface that can be very exciting at the right time. One morning I was washing clothes in the basement and my lover came up behind me, and we ended up making love 'with me half on top of the washing machine. It was sexy because it felt so urgent and passionate, as if neither of us could wait to go upstairs."

Another woman recalls an incident that began in anger and ended in wild passion. "I was standing on a street corner fuming because the man I was supposed to meet was late," she said. "Just as I was about to leave I felt a hand on my rear end. This sexy voice whispered in my ear, 'Hey, honey, got some time for a little fun?' It was my date. I said something like, 'Sure, the jerk I was waiting for hasn't shown up,' and we played the rest of the evening like a pickup. He took me to a hotel, I pranced around the room like a hooker entertaining a john, and we really got it on. I'd never done anything like that before. The funny part is, we hadn't known each other very long."

Props

An innocuous way to make room for fantasy in your lovemaking is to give the gift that you can both enjoy: sexy underwear. It's a series of small steps from having her try it on, to modeling it for you, to really getting into the mood of the moment—if that's your mutual pleasure.

Ditto erotic literature and adults-only videotapes. So long as your house doesn't look like a frighteningly well-equipped pornographic bookstore, having them on hand allows the subject to come up naturally, if either of you chooses to raise it.

The point of all this is not to manipulate your partner into doing something she really doesn't want to do, but to set the stage for some experimentation. The hardest part about getting into "let's pretend" is giving each other permission to play in the first place. Once that hurdle is overcome, your mutual imaginations can take over.

"I'll be forever grateful to Ted for having that book of tasteful nude photographs on his coffee table," a reserved bank officer remembers. "We got to looking at it one evening, and I was surprised at how arousing I found some of the pictures. Since then, we've rented blue TV movies and they never fail to excite me. I guess there's some voyeur in all of us."

A prop that intrigues many women—and threatens many men—is the vibrator. Women who never achieved orgasms in their lives have done so with vibrators. Some even complain of becoming addicted. "I don't masturbate with my fingers anymore because a vibrator is so much faster and more intense," said one woman. "Now I worry that it may turn me off men. Men don't vibrate."

Don't be afraid to introduce a vibrator into your mutual lovemaking experiences, however. Many women who learn to achieve orgasm by using a vibrator go on to climax faster and more deeply with men. "My boyfriend brought one over one night as a joke," a woman confessed. "We started fooling around with it together. He put it near my clitoris, but not touching it, and I went right through the roof. Ever since then, when he touches that magic spot, I come almost immediately."

And don't think a vibrator is just for her, either. Some couples start out by using a vibrator just as the ads show you—on each other's neck, back, shoulders—before proceeding to the really fun places.

The third eye

If women harbor some voyeurism, many also entertain some exhibitionistic fantasies as well. I was talking with a California crafts instructor who admitted that a frequent daydream involved walking down the aisle in church just as the service began, totally nude. "Nothing happens," she said, "no one does anything or looks upset. I'm just there, nude. I feel very free, and very sexy."

Although she wasn't about to act out this particular fantasy, she said she loved to perform for her lover. "Sometimes it's a striptease, sometimes I just dance in the nude for him. But the sexiest thing is taking pictures. He has a Polaroid camera and we've taken lots of pictures of each other. I can't wait until he gets a camera to hook up to his video tape recorder!"

More than two

Orgies, three-way sex, mate swapping—hot discussion topics, maybe, but not something the men and women I talked to wanted to explore personally. At the level of a purely physical sexual experience, there's no doubt that group sex can be exciting. However, whenever you introduce a third (or fourth or fifth) person into your lovemaking, you take the risk of setting up emotional dynamics you may not be prepared to deal with.

"One of the worst evenings in my life was the night I made love with my lover and a mutual male friend," one woman remembers. "The friend had just broken up with his girlfriend, and was feeling down, and what started out as an evening to comfort him ended up with all of us in bed. I didn't know whether I should respond to him or not, and my lover didn't seem quite as blasé as he seemed earlier, and it was just a mess. Maybe if the other man had been a total stranger, it would have been different, but I don't really think so."

Personal ads

For every man there's a woman, says the song. Finding "the one" through a personal ad is a powerful fantasy for many people. There's something sexily impersonal about declaring yourself in a personal ad. It allows you to bait your trap long distance, so to speak, without having to risk in-person rejection. (There is something a little passive about the process, but we'll get to that in a moment.)

Furthermore, if you really believe you can quantify your ideal true love, you can cut down on your pre-selection time by spelling out your requirements in an ad—"should be 24–33, nonsmoker, slim, love hiking and long brunches"—and trust that only those who meet them will reply. And, in fact, this is what generally happens.

I also talked with many men and women who placed personal ads containing more explicitly sexual requirements: "White male, married, looking for discreet love in the afternoon." "Black female, 37, muscular body, seeks leather lover." And so on, right up to the limits of the paper's policies.

Who writes personal ads? The answer seems to be normal, everyday people. After all, if you're tired of bars and you don't go to church and you can't crank up much enthusiasm for another Sierra Club or Young Republican get-together, your options for meeting people are limited. Why not write an ad and see who's out there you might like?

"The first time I placed an ad," said Lillian, a thirtyish woman who had been divorced for two years and was going through a post-Christmas slump, "I thought I must be a real loser. But when I confessed my dirty little secret to a few friends, I found out I was not alone. A lot of people do it."

Who answers these ads? Again, respondents seem to come in all types, with more than enough "nice" people to make it worth the effort. Lillian told me she had received twenty-seven replies to her ad. "You could tell a few were nuts," she said, "but I put seven in my 'check them out' pile. Four turned out to be men who periodically ran ads of their own. I don't see how you could run an ad very often, though, or you would never have time to deal with the responses."

Do they really work? Yes, say those who have done it. "In September I placed an ad, just to meet someone," a man reported, "and six months later I'm still seeing one of the women who answered."

The more explicitly sexual ads also seem to pay off. No matter your particular sexual fantasy, there is bound to be someone interested in participating. Do such pairings ever ripen into something more? Sometimes. One young man said he had a fantasy of going sailing in the nude with an attractive woman, suitably undressed. On a whim, he decided to place an ad in his local paper to see who might answer.

"That's how Mary and I met," he confessed, somewhat abashed. "She turned out to be more the adventurous type than a real nudist type. We did it, and it really was fun. We still sail in the nude, although now that we're more serious about each other we don't always tell people how we met."

If you want to express your fantasies through the newspaper, there are three skills you need to learn: how to write an ad, how to answer one, and how to negotiate the initial in-person meeting.

First, select a publication the type of person you're looking for is likely to read. A weekly or monthly publication is likely to be less expensive (allowing you to run a longer ad) and attract a more homogeneous readership than your local daily.

Keep it light. Don't scare people off by baring your soul, or announcing your search for a lifelong mate.

If it's general companionship you're interested in, start by suggesting an activity you would like a companion for. "B— tennis player, male, looking for female at the same level," or "Transplanted British man seeks female compatriot who knows how to pub-crawl," are the types of ads likely to generate some healthy responses.

If it's sex that's on your mind, don't hide the fact, but don't go overboard, either. One man I talked to reported great success with the single question, "Can you wake this body up?"

When it comes to answering an ad, keep in mind that whoever ran it is going to evaluate the responses meticulously. She may be more comfortable with a letter than a phone call. Tell her something about yourself. She will read your words very carefully—and also note carefully your handwriting and stationery.

The obligatory first meeting should always be held in some neutral territory where you both can feel safe. The idea is to set up something brief and informal—a cup of coffee or a drink after work—with the clear and face-saving understanding that you both have other engagements later.

At this point, your hope of no-risk sex must suffer a temporary setback. You've advertised for someone to help you live out a sexual fantasy, perhaps, but now you've got to get acquainted, face-to-face. One man, who thought he wanted a woman interested in mild bondage, found himself sitting across a table in a coffee shop from a perfectly nice, attractive young woman dressed in a fashionable suit and carrying a briefcase.

"It was weird," he said. "We both knew what we were into, and it made us really shy. I had been looking for an object, I guess, and what I found myself dealing with was a person."

Only if you want to

As this man learned, in the long run sexual fantasies are more rewarding as enrichments of existing relationships than as vehicles for getting to know someone. The brain is indeed our most erogenous zone, and the combinations of circumstances and scenarios that turn it on are infinite in their variety. As a thoughtful and imaginative lover, you can set the stage for you and your partner to explore each other's fantasies without judgment or coercion.

But it takes time to develop the mutal trust for this to happen. Once it's there, however, you are limited only by your own imagination and willingness to explore.

As one woman put it, "Jack and I playact a lot of crazy stuff. Sometimes he 'rapes' me, sometimes I put on my Frederick's of Hollywood lingerie, and we really get wild. But the best thing about it is this totally private world we've created. Once that bedroom door is closed, it's just us. Sometimes when I'm at work I laugh out loud at what people would say if they only knew."

CHAPTER TWELVE

How to Keep It Exciting

In all long-term relationships, there's a predictable progession. First comes awkwardness and concern—sometimes excruciating, and sometimes exaggerated by intense passion. Then comes the magically private time of being in love, when neither of you can do anything wrong, when your initial worries about being accepted and appreciated simply melt away in the multiple affirmations of making love.

Finally comes the period in which you both decide to expand your lives to include the other person—either through marriage, or living together, or simply out of spoken or unspoken recognition that you are a definite part of the other's life.

But then what? How does your new, comfortable state affect your sex life?

According to the happily-ever-after scenarios, nothing changes. Romance continues at the same white-hot pitch. On the one hand, we're told that passion is supposed to become deeper and more "meaningful" now. The implication is that you aren't really supposed to care quite so much about passion anymore, at least not in the same way you first did.

At the same time, however, magazines are full of articles about "rejuvenating your relationship" and "keeping your love alive." There's a frantic quality about much of this advice, as if its purpose were less to help you enhance your sexual experiences than to avoid losing your mate.

Among the people I talked to who were involved in long-term relationships, those who reported the greatest sexual satisfaction ("It really does get better and better," they insisted) had gone beyond "coming to terms" with the inevitable changes they went through. Instead, they used the very familiarity and routine that are supposed to deaden sex to make their sex lives more exciting and varied.

A big secret of their success was the ability to make their sexual experiences reflect the changes they were going through both in their separate lives and in their relationship.

"Jim and I have been together for seven years now," Moira, a San Francisco biology teacher told me. "We are different people than we were when we met, and we keep changing. We've gone in and out of periods of varying sexual intensity, but each time we reach a new peak, it seems exciting and different, because we're different. Because we're such good friends, we're able to bring our differences to bed with us, and trust that the other person will accept them."

A living-together story for the eighties

A sadder and more common experience is reflected in the story of Jack and Lisa. They have all the pieces for a life like Jim and Moira's, but have not yet assembled them to create a sexually satisfying, long-term relationship.

When Jack met Lisa, he was ready for a change. His last relationship had been long and tempestuous—lots of big scenes, lots of high-powered sex, lots of anguished soul baring. It ended four times before it really ended, and when it was finally over, Jack found himself battle-scarred and weary. No more women for a while, he told himself. At least no serious relationships.

Then Jack met Lisa. She had short, dark curly hair, like his, a tiny rounded body and crinkly gray eyes he found totally irresistible. Like Jack, Lisa was an attorney. Unlike Jack, however, she was completely dedicated to her career and determined to make a real name for herself. That suited Jack fine: with Lisa busy with her work, she would apply no pressures to "work on" the relationship. Just a lot of good times.

And so it began. The sex, at first, was fantastic. Lisa was as passionate as Jack knew she would be. She told him he was the most sensitive and imaginative lover she could have wished for.

The first time they made love was on their first date, a longish lunch at an Italian restaurant midway between their respective offices. Since it was a weekday, they had each ordered a only single glass of wine, but as they warmed to each other they found themselves moving on to a bottle of Verdicchio.

So perhaps it was the wine that made Jack mention his friend's *pied-à-terre* in town—just a block away, he said, almost never used, and with a great view. And perhaps it was the wine that prompted Lisa to bring the apartment up again, later in the lunch, after most of the crowd had cleared out and the two of them were left to polish off their zabaglione.

"I've got a key," Jack said evenly, so aware of what was about to happen that he didn't dare put any emotion in his voice. "Would you like to see it?"

"Why not?" Lisa replied, permitting herself a small grin that bubbled over into a delighted laugh. "Since I'm already this late."

The apartment, on the twentieth floor of a highrise, was really more like a hotel room than an apartment. The bed—large, considering the size of the room—was built into a mirror-banked sleeping alcove that looked out through a floor-to-ceiling window onto the city below them.

Jack went to the window to pull the curtain.

"Oh, don't," Lisa said. "It's such a wonderful view. Let's leave it open."

"Okay," Jack agreed, drawing her into his arms. "Let's."

They made love on the bed, in front of the view and half the financial district. They were each literally shaking with passion, greedy to see and know each other's bodies, oblivious to the clothes that stood in their way. Beneath Lisa's tailored silk blouse Jack found the creamy, pillowy breasts he had fantasized about all through lunch. Her skin felt warm to the touch of his hands. His lips moved across her body, bent on experiencing every plane, every hollow, every tantalizing inch.

Her urgent moans hastened his explorations. Just when he felt he could postpone intercourse no longer, Lisa put her hands to his shoulders and with a strength that surprised him pushed his body over onto the bed.

"Now let *me*," she said with a delicious grin, and proceeded to trace her tongue over his nipples, the muscles in his chest and down his stomach to his navel. With his back arched in sudden ecstasy, he could feel her mouth at the base of his penis, making little wet forays up the shaft, each one a little higher than the one before. Then he felt her mouth reach the tip, where it stayed—wet, warm, utterly still.

After what felt like minutes, while his body surged up to the outermost limits of preorgasmic excitement, she released his penis, moved astride him, and slowly lowered her body onto his. As he entered her he felt his fever pitch of excitement shift into a deeper, longer, and more languorous sensuality.

Slowly she began an even rhythm that he could feel in every part of his body. As she quickened her pace the feeling became more powerful and more focused on his penis, but every area of his body seemed to be contributing to an erotic experience he had never known was possible before. When with a sudden arch of her back Lisa gave a little cry, Jack found himself carried over the edge into a total, soul-shaking orgasm.

Jack would always look back on this moment as one of the peak experiences of his life. They had seemed magically attuned to each other. The intensity of his lust—and hers—had overridden all the awkwardness that gets in the way of the first time.

They began seeing each other all the time. At first they repeated their lunchtime experience, but taking the time for "nooners" was a luxury two busy lawyers could not afford very often. Instead, they changed the scene to her apartment during the evenings (sometimes they even managed to get out of bed long enough to see the movie they had planned on) and on weekends.

It was during the weekends that they began to get to know each other and start the process of blending their lives. If Jack had a tennis game Saturday morning, he would leave from Lisa's apartment (which was becoming increasingly crowded with more and more of his possessions) and return later to have lunch with her. If Lisa had an important case she had to work on, Jack would shop and cook for dinner. They began doing their laundry together, expanding their private world to include social engagements with a few carefully selected friends and making plans based on the unspoken assumption that they were going to have a future together.

A temporary future? A permanent future? Neither Jack nor Lisa knew at this point or even wanted to know. The greatest part of their emotional energies was focused on the moment—being in love (as they had agreed they certainly were) and deepening their sexual connection. Now, when they made love, the experience had a richness made up of equal parts passion and domestic routine. They could make love whenever they wanted to, without having to worry about arrangements, or what the other person wanted, or whether they would measure up. It seemed like the best of both worlds.

They moved in together (or rather, Jack moved into Lisa's apartment) about six months after they met. The reasons they talked about were mostly practical: Jack's rent was about to go up, he was going crazy trying to live in two places, they spent all their time together anyway.

The day he moved in, they celebrated with dinner in "their" Italian restaurant. When they returned to the apartment, they had to climb over lots of boxes to get to the bed. There they finished off their celebration with lovemaking passionate enough to reassure them both that moving in together was the right decision. Lisa drifted off to sleep thinking she would have to hire a closet-organizing service to create some more space for Jack's things. Or maybe she could get him to throw out a few of his clothes. Some, she knew, dated back to his college days.

Now let's jump ahead to a year later. Jack and Lisa were firmly ensconced in their life as a couple. It had been a year of adjustments, large and small. Lisa hadn't realized how much time Jack spent watching TV. Jack had not known just how much effort Lisa put into organizing her life so that she had time for him *and* her career, or how upset she became if she had to alter her plans. Little things, really, but they somehow had to be accommodated, at a cost of some resentment and even more loss of romantic illusion.

More important was the different directions their separate lives were taking. It was as if, having nailed down the permanency of their relationship, each felt free to devote energies to other interests. In theory, they liked this freedom. But Lisa wanted to start saving money so that she could open her own practice, while Jack wanted them to take six weeks off and bum around Europe. What did that say about their relationship?

Sometimes it seemed to Lisa that they were like two bicycle riders who could stay together only by constantly checking each other's progress. The moment they took their eyes from each other, they risked veering farther and farther off a common path.

Making love was the vehicle they both used to maintain contact and affirm the rightness of being together. It was still a powerful experience for both of them, but it too was different from before. Each of them knew that they could not realistically expect to maintain the white-hot passion of their early days. They were prepared to accept a certain routineness, much as one accepts the inevitability of gray hair, and they even managed to take some comfort in it.

But what they hadn't expected was the way the pressures of their separate lives came to roost in the bedroom. They found they were no longer so "magically attuned" as they had been. One night Lisa worked late on a case while Jack had been home since six, and after dinner he felt like making love. Lisa didn't, but, well, why not?

Or, another night, Jack came home exhausted after being out of town for a week. Lisa had prepared a romantic dinner for two as a prelude to getting reacquainted later in bed. Jack was too tired. Lisa was disappointed and even a little panicky but, in a strange way, also relieved: she had had a hard week too, and the tiny bit of resentment she felt over "having" to come home and cook hadn't put her in a very sexy mood, either.

Neither acknowledged the fears this apparent "loss of attunement" set in motion. Privately, they each considered—and then rejected—all the techniques they had read about: dirty movies, sexy negligees, bathing together in jello and whipped cream. Somehow, they all seemed too hokey, too contrived, too unnecessary. If they had to resort to such measures, they thought, maybe they should take another look at their entire relationship.

But they didn't. Instead, they tried to ignore the changes in their sexual relationship, chalking up the shift as something that sooner or later happens to all couples.

Understanding sexual urgency

The trap that Lisa and Jack fell into is very common. Once the initial rush of passion subsides, many people assume that it is dead forever, even while they secretly suspect that for other people with "better" relationships it may not be. What Lisa and Jack—and a lot of other couples—need to deal with, for starters, is the nature of sexual urgency, and what often lies behind it.

In addition to the purely (and wonderfully) physical need that leads to torn blouses, late dinners, and unanticipated locations, there is a lot of personal validation involved in sexual urgency, especially in the beginning of a relationship.

Said one woman, "I can't tell you how comforting it was to know we had this voracious appetite for each other, even when he would sometimes pressure me into having sex when I didn't feel like it. It meant to me that I was desirable, that we had a strong connection, that we were 'right' for each other. I used to entice him, sometimes, just to be sure it was still there for both of us."

In a longer-term relationship, this validation is often provided by the commitment itself. So, while the physical need may still be present, the feeling of urgency isn't quite so compelling. Sometimes this can feel as if your partner is taking you for granted, although if you were totally honest, you might admit that you don't feel quite so urgent yourself.

"At first Scott and I made love every night we slept together," a young dental assistant said. "The first night we didn't was really traumatic for me. He kissed me, turned off the light, and went to sleep, but I just lay there in a panic. I know it sounds crazy, but I thought, well, this is the beginning of the end."

It needn't be the end at all. In fact, it can mean you have shifted into a closer relationship, where you have discovered additional ways to achieve intimacy, a sense of self-worth, and a feeling of permanence.

Accept the change in this light. Resist the temptation to insist on making love simply to prove that you still love each other. That way brings eventual resentment on her part, failed erections on yours— and real danger for the relationship. At the same time, however, make sure you show her in every other way you can think of that you are still very much in love with her.

When you reach this point, all kinds of new and wonderful sexual possibilities can emerge.

For one thing, rejection won't be quite so hard to give—or take. It still may not be a barrel of laughs, but it shouldn't have quite the life-or-death quality it had before.

Think of the freedom this can bring. Knowing you and your partner can say no frees both of you from having to second-guess each other. "In the early months of our relationship, Marge and I were both eager to please," Ken said, "and we didn't like to turn each other down. We were very conservative in our sexual practices, so that we wouldn't force the other person into doing something they didn't want to. Now, because we can say no to each other more easily, we both get a lot more inventive."

Couples at this stage often make some startling discoveries about their own sexuality. They may find they like to make love less frequently than they had thought—or at different times of the day, or under different circumstances.

One woman said that only as she and her husband grew closer did she understand an internal pressure to have sex she had felt all her adult life. "It was almost like masturbating," she said. "I thought I needed sex all the time. It used to drive my husband crazy. Now I realize a lot of what I was looking for was just reassurance. When we make love now, it's because we *want* to—and it's a lot better."

Added another, "I could never understand when

my boyfriend wanted a 'quickie.' For me, making love had to be romantic all the time. But you know, every once in a while a quickie is great—no emotional statement, just a very, very physical experience. As long as I know the other is there, I can really get into being a sexual animal.''

How to keep stress out of the bedroom

Like Jack and Lisa, couples in a long-term relationship find that their lives quickly become intertwined. This was their intent, after all; it's almost the definition of adult intimacy.

But often they are not prepared for the impact on their sex lives. When they were first getting acquainted, making love was precious, fragile, separate, special. They worked to keep it that way; they *needed* to keep it that way until they were sure it was strong enough to withstand more exposure.

If the relationship is going anywhere, however, sooner or later begins the imperceptible process of merging lives—and the stresses that go with it. One night you realize you're not just making love to a woman with incredibly soft skin and alabaster thighs. She is also the woman who has started to worry that your smoking will shorten your life, or is trying to do something about her dead-end career, or wants to go to the beach while you want to go to the mountains— and on and on. Small wonder that the passion that once came so quickly now must often be coaxed and cajoled, and even then does not always appear.

When this happens, what can you do?

First of all, don't define the problem as sexual. It's really much broader. Thinking of it in purely sexual terms will only increase the stresses you both feel. It may also lead you into desperate attempts at jazzing up your sex life. Although there's nothing wrong with adding variety to your lovemaking routine (and we'll get to this in a moment), until the circumstances are right, your efforts are bound to fail.

Instead, try comforting. "Comforting" may not sound very sexy, but these days couples need all they can get. Let her know you understand the problems she may be going through. Do what you can to help. Reassure her that you still love her, even though neither of you may feel like making love at that very moment.

Next, spend some time making your bedroom a special place. This has its practical *and* emotional aspects. For example, just as you can agree not to bring up stressful topics at the dinner table, you can agree not to discuss them in bed.

You can also make some physical changes in the bedroom itself to create a more soothing and nurturing environment. One couple I spoke to decided to put up some new curtains that would let in the light but also provide privacy. "We like to make love during the day," the woman said, "but with the curtains drawn it looked too dark and tacky."

If you've got the room, you might want to add a couple of easy chairs to make a sort of bedroom suite. Creating your own private sitting-and-talking area is especially important if children are around. It enables the two of you to have private time together that can flow naturally into making love, if you both feel like it.

Put a lock on the bedroom door, and use it. This simple solution may go farther toward removing worry and concern than any other single thing you do. Said one mother, "The kids know that my husband and I need the time together, not just for making love, but for staying connected. Some days that lock on the door can mean the difference between marriage and divorce."

How to create new sexual excitements

Let's say you remove the impediments to lovemaking that may have slowly crept into your life. You may find that setting them aside is all you need to bring back the kind of lovemaking you enjoyed when you first met.

On the other hand, you may want more—not out of sexual boredom, as so many people fear, but out of the very basic human need to grow and change.

A great deal of sexual boredom sets in when sex is no longer the sole validator and contact point in a relationship. This means there is no longer such a big risk in making love and also less of a payoff when you are successful. Less risk, less excitement.

The answer to enhancing your sexual excitement, then, is to find ways to take risks that will add newness and increase the payoffs—and keep the two of you alive and growing.

Change the scene

At the lower end of the risk spectrum is going away for the weekend, or even just for overnight. Added to the advantage of getting away from pressures at home is the promise of the new and unknown.

Anticipation, in fact, may be the greatest aphrodisiac. "Once my husband surprised me with two airline tickets to Puerto Vallarta for the next weekend," one woman said. 'Don't even pack,' he told me. 'You can buy what you need when we get there.' It was wonderful, but I missed having the time to look forward to the trip."

Said another woman, "I always like to have a trip scheduled, even if it's two or three months in advance. I play out little scenarios in my mind—like what I'll wear the first night at dinner, what the room will look like, what my husband and I will do in bed, what the maid will say when she comes in. I can work up a real tingle."

For many couples, simply being alone together in an unfamiliar hotel room adds a certain spice. "You know what I think is sexy?" one woman admitted with a shy grin. "Seeing my boyfriend and me reflected in the bathroom mirror of a hotel room, half-dressed, getting ready to go out for dinner. Maybe it's the different lighting, but it really turns me on to see us reflected together. We look like us, but a sexier us."

Reverse roles

When you and your partner were first getting to know each other's bodies, you went to great lengths to find out what she liked. Did she go crazy when you put your tongue in her navel? Did she like you to pay a lot of attention to her toes? Was oral sex a requirement for orgasm?

Having by now presumably found out what turns her on, you may see no need to do any more research. This is a mistake. You have changed. *She* has changed. You are both more relaxed with each other now; you know your own bodies better. You know what you like now and what you don't.

A wonderful nonverbal way to share this information with each other is to reverse roles. Here's how it works. Tell your partner you're going to pleasure her as if she were you. Touch her in all the places *you* would like to be touched, kiss her the way *you* would like to be kissed, proceed at the pace *you* would like to proceed.

Then allow her to do the same to you. This can be a marvelously nonthreatening means for couples who thought they knew each other's every sexual "do and don't" to become reacquainted—as the people they are *now*. "It worked for us," Susan, a long-legged runner, reported. "We would have felt awkward and critical sitting down and saying what we were able to communicate in bed without words. Besides, there aren't always words for what you mean in those areas."

Assert yourself

Close to the upper end of the risk spectrum is making a direct statement of what you want or don't want. The risk, of course, is getting turned down, or thought less of in some way. People in a long-term relationship have usually arranged to minimize the occasions when they have to stick their necks out. After a while, certain gestures or phrases—or times—take on special private meanings that are never directly acknowledged: "I want to make love tonight," or "Not tonight, dear," or "This is going to be a quickie," or "I'm not really interested, but I don't mind that you are," or "If this is Saturday, it must mean sex."

There's nothing wrong with this kind of sexual shorthand—it's testimony, in fact, to the closeness you have achieved—except that it can kill off the excitement that you experienced when you first began to make love and never knew exactly what would happen. You may feel a certain comfort in the risk-free communication you have established. Or you may have reached the point where this comforting routine has turned stale.

Many couples who reach this stage assume it is time to bring out the chains, vibrators, kinky underwear, and all the other trappings that they have been told will create a renewed feeling of excitement. Well, maybe, but you really don't have to go to such extremes to achieve the same effect.

Try some direct statements that let your partner know just what you are feeling and what you would like to do about it. For example, instead of simply assuming you will make love at the end of the day, as usual, call her up in the middle of the afternoon. "I've been thinking about making love with you all day," you might say. "How about if I got some champagne and came home a little early tonight?" In this way, you've created some anticipation, suggested something new, declared your feelings, and set the stage for the unpredictable to happen.

A man I talked to claims the secret to keeping sexual excitement in a relationship is never taking anything for granted. "It's always better if you ask for it," he says, "and you know she's not going to say yes unless she really wants to."

And if she says no?

"That's part of the game," he replied. "It keeps you on your toes—being inventive, figuring out what would make her say yes, being sensitive to her needs in the moment. And you can say no too, you know. It keeps an element of pursuit in the relationship. We both like that."

What about jealousy?

Tops on the list of risk taking in your relationship is injecting a note of jealousy. Showing some interest in another woman—or realizing that your partner may be attracted to another man—is a sure way to throw your relationship off balance.

Nobody in his right mind would suggest using jealousy as a calculated ploy to create excitement. In the first place, it's too hurtful, too manipulative, and too dishonest to have any place in a truly loving relationship. Furthermore, there's no telling where it might lead. If you decide to up the ante by paying extravagant attention to a woman you find attractive, your partner may decide to respond in kind with another man. This mutual escalation could eventually produce feelings of anger and betrayal strong enough to kill off the relationship altogether.

On the other hand, to keep from taking each other for granted, it's important for both of you to know you are sexual creatures attracted—and attractive—to others.

The dilemma, of course, comes in knowing where to draw the line. The best answer is to take your cue from your relationship. If it feels complete and satisfying to both of you, then you can probably attend a party and engage in some harmless flirtations without causing any problems. "It gives me a thrill when other women find John attractive," one woman told me. "I feel proud that he's mine. I don't blame him for responding to them—a little. I'd do the same in his position. It keeps the juices flowing between us."

Problems arise, however, if you find yourself responding to other women in ways you don't with your mate. If she sees this happening, she will feel hurt and resentful. As one woman put it, "I used to be involved with a guy who was very quiet and laid back—until he met some woman at a party, and then he'd start getting very witty and charming. It made me furious that I wasn't getting any of that. I guess he thought he didn't have to make the effort with me."

Does marriage make it different?

These days, a big question for many couples who are living together and considering marriage is: how will marriage affect our love life?

Among the couples I talked to, the consensus was "not much." A lot of the research on the subject indicates that the big changes come in the setting up of a single household rather than the legalities of the union itself.

The biggest exception to this finding—and for some people it's significant—has to do with how being a husband or a wife makes people *feel*. As one woman put it, "When Tom and I were living together, I had no problem being my own person. When we first got married, though, I started thinking of myself as a *wife*, with all I assumed that implied. It took me awhile to realize I could be a wife and me at the same time."

CHAPTER THIRTEEN

What to Do About Problems

Therapists will tell you that most of their patients are women. Men resist admitting they have serious personal problems, and resist even more the notion that they need help in solving them. Yet no one can deny a man's problems when it comes to sexual performance. A penis is either erect or it isn't. A man can either exert some measure of control over when he ejaculates or he can't.

When a man experiences performance problems, he suffers, his relationship suffers, and the woman in his life is thrown into an emotional turmoil of her own. "Is it me?" she may ask herself. "Maybe he no longer finds me attractive. Maybe I'm doing something—or not doing something—that's causing his problem."

"My lover went through a period when he had trouble getting erections, and I felt totally helpless," a Marin County legal assistant told me. "I told him it really didn't matter to me, but because I could see how much it mattered to him, I tried every technique I could think of to help him out. Nothing seemed to work. And the more I tried, the more it seemed *I* was the one who wanted the erection, which only made things worse. It was terrible. Finally, I just backed off. We didn't have sex for a month, and after that things sort of returned to normal. But neither of us has ever really talked about it."

Aside from certain debilitating physical conditions, men's sexual problems are rooted, by and large, in nonphysical causes. The symptoms may be the same—

failure to get or keep an erection, premature ejaculation—but the causes can vary widely. In some cases, professional help may be required to determine what's going on, especially if it's been going on for some time. But there are also questions you can ask yourself that may produce some answers you can take action on.

(1) Have you created a vicious cycle?

At some time or other, all men experience difficulties in the area of sexual performance. They can't get an erection when they want one, or their erection doesn't last, or they ejaculate too soon. So, no big deal. It happens to everyone, and besides, tomorrow is another day.

But if it happens again, or at some "worst possible moment," or during a period of general self-doubt, it can cease to be just a "performance difficulty." Now it becomes a psychological lightning rod, attracting a free-floating series of self-punishing fears: "I can't perform, I'm not a real man, I am useless, powerless ... impotent." The more these fears are activated and attached to the arena of sexual performance, the more difficult it becomes to perform. Which, of course, only fuels the self-doubt.

To stop this vicious cycle, you need to take the pressure off yourself. The first step in the process is to stop trying. Let your partner know what's happening with you. This is easier said than done, but by explaining your feelings and fears to her you will not only relieve her of the burden of feeling inadequate, but you will be enlisting her help. This is help you will need and which she will be happy to give. "When my boyfriend was finally able to talk about it, I felt so relieved," one woman said. "It was a moment of real closeness for us."

Adopt a no-sex rule for a while. Not "no cuddling," or "no touching," just no intercourse. Spend a few evenings together in bed, working up gradually to caressing and manual manipulation. Ignore your erections. Resist the temptation to rush into action. The whole idea is to take off any pressure to perform; this is the pressure that has stymied you. Once you stop trying to will erections, they will come unbidden. In the meantime, you can take the opportunity to enrich and expand your lovemaking capabilities, free from the need to rush to orgasm.

(2) Do you tune in to YOUR sexual mood?

"In the pursuit of sex, men make demands on their bodies of an order of magnitude they would not think of making on their automobiles," says a San Francisco psychiatrist. "They totally buy in to the idea that real men are always ready for sex—at any time, under any circumstances. These same men may go to great lengths to tune in to a woman's sexual mood, but they never think of doing the same for themselves. They can end up by pushing themselves beyond their ability to perform."

The truth is, men have their moods too, even the most studly. They may be too tired, or too preoccupied, or simply may not feel like having sex at that particular moment. Gently declining a partner's advances may feel rude or unmanly, but if you are clear about your reasons, she will understand. It will also prevent her from taking your refusal as a comment on your feelings about her.

As one woman admitted, "I guess part of being liberated means learning how to deal with rejection, like men have had to do. I can't say I like it, but it's better than having him get into something he doesn't really want to do, and then not be able to do it. Then he feels bad, and I feel bad."

Besides, "no" to intercourse doesn't have to mean

"no" to a massage, or a hot tub, or just being held. And if, in the course of receiving a lot of tenderness and nurturing, you change your mind, the experience is likely to be more fulfilling for both of you.

Henry, an idealistic young Washington lawyer, considered himself far beyond the macho attitudes he saw—and disapproved of—in his father. But when he and Susan ran into some sexual problems, he had to take another look. "I wasn't macho in the sense of patronizing women," he said. "But I had the idea that I always had to master whatever challenge I faced, and I carried that feeling over into sex."

Said Susan, "I played into it. I thought that liberated women were supposed to ask for sex whenever they wanted it. But that only works if the man is allowed to say no."

Added Henry, "I guess I hadn't learned that particular rule. Now I'm a little better at it."

"And," said Susan, "I'm a little better at reading his mood."

(3) Are you sitting on some unexpressed feelings?

Unspoken feelings, often of an angry nature, can be very effective erection preventers. That's one reason a good fight can end with both of you making passionate love.

"Many men unconsciously withhold themselves from their partners by failing to get an erection," a psychotherapist told me. "Without being aware of what they are doing, they adopt an attitude of 'I'll fix you. If it's sex you want, I won't give it to you.' Once they find more direct ways to express their feelings, their impotence problems vanish."

This is not to say that you must turn your bedroom into a boxing ring. A better approach is to do your best to stay current with your partner and bring up whatever is upsetting you before it reaches the point of a knock-down, drag-out battle. "We've had some marathon talks where I could hardly stay awake," a man told me, "but we don't close down to each other anymore. And our lovemaking is a lot better now. I used to think that no matter what the problem was, we could make it go away by going to bed. Now I know that's not always true."

One way to tell if you are harboring unexpressed anger is to examine your general attitude toward your partner. Do you find yourself carrying on unspoken fights with her all the time? Does everything about her often seem to irritate you? Do you explode in flashes of anger that don't clear the air? Chances are there may be larger issues you need to deal with.

As one man said, "I've got my pet peeves, like everybody else. But one day I realized I really shouldn't care quite so much which way she put in a new roll of toilet paper. So I told her just that, and she said, 'Well, what's the problem?' That got us started talking. I felt one hundred percent better afterward."

(4) Are you seeking sex for all the wrong reasons?

When sex flows naturally from your feelings of closeness and love for your partner, it is effortless. When you use sex to achieve other ends, sooner or later you may find you have pushed your body beyond its emotional limits, and it will refuse to respond to your demands any longer.

There are several common sexual patterns men fall into which have little to do with their feelings. Normal in moderation, these elements can be disastrous in excess.

To prove your masculinity

Although most men find a very satisfying affirmation of their masculinity in the act of making love, seeing it only in these terms is another matter altogether. Such men are the bed hoppers, the leerers, and the locker-room orators.

They may also be more than a little jealous. One disenchanted woman described her experience with a man who was unsure of his masculinity. "He always made a point of noticing other women—making remarks, ostentatiously turning his head—but if I so much as noticed another man, he got sulky. Then, he invariably wanted to make love, as if he would show me just who the better man was. Some of the time, though, he couldn't get an erection, and then he really felt terrible."

To alleviate boredom

No one denies that making love can be exciting, or that it offers sensations and experiences you can get nowhere else. But going after sex simply as a distraction is ultimately a deadening and self-defeating pursuit.

Tuck, a young college teacher in Seattle, woke up to this fact almost by accident. "My life was on hold," he said. "Did I want to go back to graduate school? Did I want to switch careers? What I did was spend a lot of time in bars, chasing women. It was fun, everybody else was doing it, so why not?"

"Why not" for Tuck, and a lot of other people, turned out to be a fear of genital Herpes. "I started staying home, instead of hitting the bars every night," he said. "It was only then I realized that sex for me had become a way of filling time, of avoiding what I didn't want to face. Now I'm more discriminating. I'm getting my career in order, and my love life is looking up too."

To "make it better"

Making love is a powerful form of communication, but it is no cure-all. Sometimes you must talk things out. There are times when making love, no matter how skilled you may be, cannot bridge the differences between you and your partner or provide her what she needs. Says one expert on human behavior, "Men are programmed to lump their needs for closeness and love under sex. To them, making love is a way of expressing these needs and having them met. The problem is that women often see this behavior as further proof that all men are after sex, and sex only."

To dominate

The male fantasy of using sex to dominate women and bring them under his control is more than a little reminiscent of a stallion with his harem of mares. However, while the feeling of being dominated excites many women, as a primary motivator for making love, it's a killer for men and a turnoff for their partners.

"I love to turn to jelly at my lover's touch," one woman said, "but not when it becomes a power struggle, and certainly not when I get the impression I'm a notch on his bedpost."

Added a man, "I ran into sexual problems by seeing every woman I wanted to meet as a challenge. The more independent she was, the more I wanted to get her. The whole process was a sexual turn-on for me, until the time when I was in bed with a woman and couldn't get an erection—and didn't even care. I suddenly realized I had just been going through the motions."

If your problem is premature ejaculation

Unlike erection problems, the matter of premature ejaculation is relative. If a man ejaculates after ten minutes of intercourse, some women may still feel he may have come "too soon." It boils down to the ability to maintain a satisfactory degree of control over timing so that neither you nor your partner feels disappointed.

The standard technique has always been to "think about something else," an approach that neither men nor women find altogether to their liking. As one man said, "If I wanted to plan next week's sales conference, there are better times and places to do it. Besides, that's not why I make love in the first place."

Echoes a woman, "It's depersonalizing to think that while my lover and I are locked in a passionate embrace, he's going over the basics of his golf swing, or making out a shopping list. I want him with me—mind, body, and soul."

Fortunately, sex researchers have now developed a relatively simple exercise called the "squeeze technique" that can virtually eliminate the problem of premature ejaculation.

Start by lying on your back, with your partner facing you. Ask her to stimulate your penis until you feel orgasm is near. Just before you are about to lose control, signal her to stop and have her squeeze your penis just beneath the tip—hard enough to cause you to lose your erection but not hard enough to hurt. Then repeat the process, once again having her squeeze your penis just before orgasm.

Then proceed to intercourse, if possible with your partner astride you. Just before orgasm, withdraw (or have her lift up) and ask her to apply pressure with her fingers just below the tip of your penis. According to Masters and Johnson, this simple approach cured almost all of one group of their patients in two weeks' time. It's behavior modification, and its purpose it to give the man a sense of control over when he ejaculates.

What a therapist can do for you

In some circles the idea of seeking psychological counseling still has shameful overtones of mental illness. Furthermore, many people avoid therapy out of a fear that it will be long-term, expensive, and deeply introspective.

Fortunately, however, a new breed of therapist now takes a different tack. "I look on myself as a kind of emotional consultant," a young therapist in San Francisco said. "I see people with specific emotional problems, in much the same way a lawyer sees people with specific legal problems. I offer them my assessment of the problem, and sometimes that's all they need. Of course, in other cases, they may want to return for further sessions. But I don't start out assuming that therapy is going to be long-term. And usually it isn't."

Perhaps the major contribution a therapist can make is a qualified outsider's point of view on your problem. This is especially true if you have gotten yourself into a vicious cycle in which failure begets self-doubt which begets more failure. One man said his failure to achieve erections had become obsessional. "What the therapist did was to unravel all that, and get me to see how hard I was being on myself in all areas of my life, not just sex. I had to learn how to give myself permission to fail before I could succeed."

If you have a sexual problem, should you see a therapist who specializes in sexual problems?

Not necessarily. The most important criterion in your selection should be how comfortable you feel with whomever you select, including whether the person is a man or a woman. Said the San Francisco therapist, "The process of selecting a therapist isn' very scientific. I advise people to shop around and go with the one they like. Don't let yourself be bullied or manipulated into staying with someone you don't feel compatible with. No matter how good they may be, they won't be right for you."

"Making love"

The ultimate test of any therapy—and, in fact, of all your efforts to become a more skilled and sensitive lover—will be the effect on your ability to give and receive love. Your initial task may be to learn the techniques. Your ultimate challenge is to reach the point where you can forget them.

In a sense, at first it's a little like learning a sport. You practice and practice on isolated movements, concentrating on form and strategy—until the time arrives when everything seems to come together in a glorious fusion and you lose yourself in the experience.

You will know you have reached this point when "making love" ceases to be a euphemism for "having sex" and instead describes an experience in which you and your partner discover and express through physical intimacy the love you feel for each other. Sexual gymnastics are very much a thing of the past. Sexual intimacy is how the best feelings—and the best times— happen. In the long run, isn't that what sex is all about?